D0645922

The Wise Book of Whys

TodayIFoundOut.com

Produced by Vacca Foeda Media, LLC
P.O. Box 1011, Gold Bar, WA 98251 U.S.A.

ISBN-10: 1494337223
ISBN-13: 978-1494337223

In instances where trademarked names are used in this book, where Vacca Foeda Media is aware of a trademark claim, the names appear starting with a capital letter.

DEDICATION

The practice of dedicating books to some person or organization has been around seemingly as long as there have been books. In many of the earliest instances, this was not only used to honor patrons of the author, but even sometimes as a way for writers to earn extra money by accepting funds from someone who simply wanted to appear in the published work's dedication, often with gratuitous affection.

As writing books and other works became more lucrative, particularly in the last few centuries, this practice gradually died out in favor of dedicating books to individuals of particular importance to the author.

With that said, I would like to dedicate this book to my wife, Verity, who only paid me a little for this mention.

Daven Hiskey
Gold Bar, Washington
November 2013

CONTENTS

WHY ONE BAD APPLE SPOILS A BUNCH

This isn't just a popular metaphor, it's actually true. One bad apple will absolutely quickly spoil an entire box of apples. The obvious way this can happen is simply if one of the apples is infested with some fungi or critters that reproduce and spread throughout all the apples in a box, ruining them as they go.

The less obvious, but perhaps even more common, way this can happen has to do with a hydrocarbon chemical known as ethylene. Ethylene is a hormone produced and released into the air by most plants, including from the fruit of certain plants, such as apples, bananas, pears, etc.

So what does this have to do with one "bad" apple? The "bad" apple is usually one that is wounded in some way or is otherwise overripe. As a consequence to the wound on the apple, or if it's just already very ripe, the apple in question will give off significantly more ethylene than normal. That ethylene accelerates the ripening process in the apples around it, which causes them to give off more ethylene, further accelerating the ripening process in all the apples in the box. In very short order, the entire box of apples will be overripe and eventually unpalatable for eating.

Humans have actually been using ethylene to control ripening processes since before we knew about the hormone. The first known instance of this was in ancient Egypt where they would slash figs and place them with other fruits and vegetables in order to accelerate the ripening process, with the wound stimulating the production of relatively large amounts of ethylene.

Today, ethylene is popularly used by banana distributors to partially ripen the fruit before the final distribution to stores. Bananas are picked when they are quite green and hard. They are shipped this way to allow them to be in transit for longer periods, as well as reduce the chances of bruising during transport. Once they are at the local distribution warehouses, they are often exposed to ethylene gas in a closed chamber for 24-48 hours to drastically accelerate the ripening process, making them ready for store shelves.

BONUS FACT

Even if un-wounded, bananas put off large amounts of ethylene, relative to many other fruits. In fact, if you'd like to speed up the ripening of some green bananas or other fruit or vegetables, put them in a paper bag together overnight. The trapped ethylene will quickly ripen the fruit, and the paper bag will still let enough oxygen in to keep the ripening process going smoothly. On the same token, putting fresh bananas in the same container as an overripe banana will drastically accelerate the ripening process of the fresh bananas, which is already quite a fast process.

On the flipside, if you want to slow the ripening of bananas, put them in the refrigerator. Contrary to what you might think from seeing the bananas rapidly turn to brown and then black when placed in a refrigerator, this drastically slows the internal ripening process of the fruit. The skin will look like the banana is rotten, but the inside will stay tasty for up to about a week. So wait until a hand of bananas reaches the perfect ripeness, then plop them in your fridge to lock them in that state for about a week. No more bothering with the tiny window of eating opportunity normally presented by bananas left on the kitchen counter.

WHY THE MASS AVOIDANCE OF SOME BUSINESS IS CALLED "BOYCOTTING"

This term was named after a nineteenth century Englishman, Captain Charles C. Boycott (who originally had the surname "Boycatt," but the family changed the spelling when he was nine years old). If you guessed that at a certain point Captain Boycott became quite unpopular with the masses, you're correct.

Shortly before Boycott would find himself boycotted, the situation in Ireland was that just .2% of the population owned almost every square inch of land in Ireland. Most of the owners of the land also didn't live in Ireland but simply rented their land out to tenant farmers, generally on one-year leases.

In the mid-nineteenth century, many of these tenant farmers banded together with three goals: "Fair Rent, Fixity of Tenure, and Free Sale". One particular organization that emerged in the 1870s pushing these "Three F's," among other things, was the Irish National Land League.

This brings us to September of 1880. The leader of the Land League, Parliament member Charles Stewart Parnell, was giving a speech to many of the members of that organization. During the speech, after the crowd, in true mob-like fashion, expressed that any tenant farmer who bids on an evicted neighbor's land should be killed, Parnell humbly suggested that another tact should be used.

Rather than murder the individual, he proposed it would be more Christian to simply "shun him on the fair green and in the market place, and even in the place of worship, by leaving him alone, by putting him in moral Coventry, by isolating him from the rest of the country, as if he were the leper of old – you must show him your detestation of the crime he committed."

Essentially, they were to be boycotted, but they didn't have that term yet, though they wouldn't have to wait long. The first documented reference of "Boycott" being used as a verb was just two weeks after that speech.

At the time, Captain Charles Boycott, now retired from the military, was working as a land manager for the third Earl of Erne, John Crichton. The harvest that year wasn't turning out well for many farmers, so as a concession to tenants, Boycott decided to reduce their rent by 10%. Rather than accept this, his tenants demanded a 25% reduction, which Boycott's boss, the Earl of Erne, refused. In the end, 11 of the Earl's tenants didn't pay their rent.

Thus, a mere three days after this speech, Boycott began the process of serving eviction notices to those who hadn't paid, sending out the Constabulary to do this. Needless to say, this did not go over well with the already riled up masses.

Upon the tenants realizing eviction notices were going out, the women of the area began throwing things such as rocks and manure at those delivering the notices until the Constabulary left without being able to serve all the notices to the head of the households, which was required by law for the eviction notice to be considered served. Without the notices delivered, nobody had to leave their homes.

Next, the teaming masses decided to use Parnell's proposed social ostracism against Boycott and anyone who worked under him. Soon, those who worked under Boycott began leaving his service, often with those workers being coerced and threatened by others until they, too, joined in the ostracizing of Boycott.

This ultimately left Boycott with a large estate to manage, but no workers to farm the remainder of the crops. Other businesses also stopped being willing to do business with Boycott; he couldn't even buy food locally and getting it from afar was difficult as carriage drivers, ship captains, and letter handlers on the whole wouldn't work with him.

In late November, this led to Boycott being forced to leave his home, fleeing to Dublin. Even there, he was met with hostility and businesses that were willing to serve him were threatened with being "boycotted."

The practice of boycotting spread, and within a decade whenever a business did something to the dislike of the Irish National Land League, the business would quickly find themself boycotted, with the name for the practice sticking due to the wide publication of Boycott's plight in the news. By 1888, just eight years after Boycott was first boycotted, the word even made it into the *New English Dictionary on Historical Principles*, better known today as the *Oxford English Dictionary*.

The word spread to other European languages and quickly

made it over to America when Captain Boycott visited friends in Virginia, attempting to do so in secret -registering under the name "Charles Cunningham." The newspapers caught wind of his arrival anyway and widely publicized his history, which got the term firmly planted in American English as well.

BONUS FACT

Boycott did get his crops harvested the year he was boycotted, finding 50 workers from out of town to come harvest his crops. The problem was that the locals did not take kindly to this, so the government had to step in and had nearly one thousand soldiers escort the workers and protect them while they worked. Funny enough, this ended up costing the British government about £10,000. How much were the crops worth? About £500.

WHY THE SPEED OF SEAFARING VESSELS IS MEASURED IN KNOTS

How fast you're going while out floating on the big blue can be notoriously tricky to judge if you're just eyeballing it. One method used to get around this issue was introduced in the sixteenth century using a "chip log" or "log-line."

In a nutshell, this method used a plank of wood (usually wedge shaped and weighted on one end so it would float perpendicular to the water to increase drag) tied to a long thin line that had knots tied at evenly spaced intervals.

The wood would be tossed into the water and the line let out while a sailor used a sand-glass to time the number of knots let out in the given timespan. As for the interval and the time-span, this varied somewhat in the beginning, but for reference, one mid-eighteenth century version (attested in *A Voyage to South America* by Jorge Juan and Antonio de Ulloa) had the knots at 1/120th of a mile with a 30-second timer.

This has all since been standardized based on the nautical mile (today equaling 1.852 kilometers). One knot then equals one nautical mile per hour. In landlubber terms, this is about 1.15 miles per hour or 1.852 kilometers per hour. More pertinently, this is equal to 1/60th a degree of latitude or longitude or one minute of arc (assuming the Earth is a perfect sphere, which it's not -being squashed at the poles and bulging in the middle -but this is a good enough approximation). Thus, if you were traveling at one knot, it would take you approximately 60 hours to go 1 degree of longitude or latitude.

So, today, if you're using a 28-second timer, to get your accurate speed in knots, you need to have the interval of knots at 14.4018 meters (47 feet, 3 inches). The number of knots that are unrolled during that span is your speed in knots.

BONUS FACT

Before "knots" a common way to measure a ship's speed was simply to drop a log or other floating object into the water at the front of a ship, then time how long it took for it to reach the back of the ship. Your speed could then be calculated using this time and the known length of the ship.

WHY "AULD LANG SYNE" IS COMMONLY SUNG ON NEW YEAR'S EVE

This tradition is mostly thanks to Guy Lombardo and the Royal Canadian Band. While their work is largely unknown by those born in the last few decades, the band has sold over 300 million records to date. Guy Lombardo himself has three stars on the Hollywood Walk of Fame, and he was once the "Dick Clark" of New Years before Clark and his "New Year's Rockin' Eve," attempting to appeal to younger audiences, started supplanting "Mr. New Year's Eve," Guy Lombardo.

It was in 1929 that Guy Lombardo and his band took the stage at the Roosevelt Hotel in New York City on New Year's Eve. Their performance that night was being broadcast on the radio, before midnight Eastern-time on CBS, then after on NBC radio.

At midnight, as a transition between the broadcasts, the song they chose to play was an old Scottish folk song Lombardo had first heard from Scottish immigrants in Ontario. The song was Auld Lang Syne.

Previous to this, there are several documented instances of others singing this song on New Year's Eve, going all the way back to the mid-nineteenth century, but it wasn't anywhere close to the staple it would soon be after Lombardo's performance.

The next year, and every year thereafter, all the way to 1976, with Lombardo dying at the age of 75 in 1977, they played it at midnight on New Year's Eve at first broadcast out on the radio and later on TV. Thanks to "Mr. New Year's Eve" and his band, it's still tradition to this day.

BONUS FACT

It is often said that the song, *Auld Lang Syne*, was written by famed eighteenth century poet/songwriter, "Scotland's Favorite Son" -Robert Burns. However, Burns never claimed to have written the song -in fact, quite the opposite. When he submitted it to the *Scots Musical Museum*, he included a note stating: "The following song, an old song, of the olden times, and which has never been in print, nor even in manuscript until I took it down from an old man's singing, is enough to recommend any air."

The song was first published in 1788, and later a slightly modified version was published in Thomson's Select Songs of Scotland in 1799, three years after Burns' death.

The title, roughly translated to modern English, literally means "old long since," but more figuratively means, "Times Gone By" or "Times Long Past." It is simply a song about remembering old friends and the times spent with them. Burns set the lyrics to a traditional Scottish ditty called *Can Ye Labour Lea*.

WHY CASHEWS ARE NOT SOLD TO CONSUMERS IN THEIR SHELLS

Cashews are a member of the same family as poison ivy, Anacardiaceae. Like poison ivy and many other members of the family, part of the cashew plant contains an oily chemical called urushiol, which is a strong irritant for most people and can even be fatal for some if ingested.

In cashews, the urushiol is found not only in the leaves, but also in a layer of oil between the shell and the cashew seed. Needless to say, shelling cashews is something that needs to be done very carefully and not by consumers.

Despite the need for care in shelling cashews, it's still often done by hand, much to the chagrin of the workers involved, particularly in poorer nations where safety equipment is often lacking.

From the above, you might be wondering why you can purchase raw cashews. It turns out, even so-called "raw" cashews are not actually raw. Eating true raw, unprocessed cashew seeds would result in you ingesting some of this urushiol, which, as mentioned, can potentially be fatal. Thus, the seeds must either be roasted at high temperatures to destroy the offending oil or, in the case of "raw" cashews, usually steamed and/or boiled in oils.

BONUS FACT

Unlike many seeds, the cashew seed actually grows on the outside of the fruit itself, making it a "false fruit" or "accessory fruit." The fruit, known as a cashew apple, is actually very good to eat, but is not widely consumed outside of areas it is grown in due to the fact that it's not easy to transport because of its extremely fragile skin.

WHY SOME ENGLISH SPEAKING COUNTRIES PRONOUNCE "Z" AS "ZED" AND OTHERS AS "ZEE"

The vast majority of the English speaking world pronounces "z" as "zed." The primary exception, of course, is in the United States where "z" is pronounced "zee."

The British and others pronounce "z," "zed," owing to the origin of the letter "z" -the Greek letter "Zeta." This gave rise to the Old French "zede," which resulted in the English "zed" around the fifteenth century.

As to why people in the United States call "z," "zee," this is likely simply adopted from the pronunciation of the letters "bee," "cee," "dee," "eee," "gee," "pee," "tee," and "vee."

The first known instance of "zee" being recorded as the correct pronunciation of the letter "z" was in Lye's New Spelling Book, published in 1677. There still was a variety of common pronunciations in North America after this, but by the nineteenth century, this changed in the United States with "zee" firmly establishing itself thanks to Daniel Webster putting his seal of approval on it in 1827, and, of course, the *Alphabet Song* copyrighted in 1835, rhyming "z" with "me."

Because of the *Alphabet Song*, the pronunciation of "z" as "zee" has started to spread, much to the chagrin of elementary school teachers the English-speaking world over. This has resulted in them often having to re-teach children the "correct" pronunciation of "z" as "zed," with the children having previously learned the song and the letter the American English way from such shows as *Sesame Street*.

Naturally, kids are generally resistant to this change owing to the fact that "tee, u, vee, w, x, y and zed, Now I know my A-B-Cs, Next time won't you sing with me" just doesn't quite sound as cohesive as "tee/vee/zee/me."

BONUS FACT

The *Alphabet Song* is based on the French *Ah, vous dirai-je, maman*, which popped up in 1761, and a couple decades later Mozart used it in his *Twelve Variations on Ah, vous dirai-je, maman*. This tune is also used for such children's songs as *Twinkle, Twinkle, Little Star* and *Baa, Baa, Black Sheep*.

WHY ROCK 'N' ROLL MUSIC IS CALLED ROCK 'N' ROLL

The word "roll" has been used since the Middle-Ages to refer to, among other things, having sex. (e.g. "Let's go for a roll in the hay" "Rolling under the sheets"). The word "rock," again among other things, has been used since the seventeenth century as a term meaning "shake or disturb." By the nineteenth century, this had also spread to black gospel singers using "rock" to refer to being shaken in a spiritual sense, as in spiritual rapture (rocked).

By the early twentieth century "rock" had evolved somewhat to being used as a slang term by black Americans referring to dancing to music with a strong beat, principally what we know of today as rhythm and blues -at the time called "Race Music" or "Race Records."

Around this same time, these two terms, "rock" and "roll," began being used together, forming a double entendre, typically referring to very suggestive or scandalous dancing as well as simply having sex. One example of this can be found in the 1922 song *My Man Rocks Me, with One Steady Roll.*

Another early reference to the term "rock and roll" was in a 1935 J. Russel Robinson lyric from Henry "Red" Allen's *Get Rhythm in Your Feet and Music in Your Soul,* "If Satan starts to hound you, commence to rock and roll. Get rhythm in your feet and music in your soul..."

This finally brings us to why Rock 'n' Roll music is called that. In the early 1950s, a Cleveland, Ohio disk jockey named Alan Freed on his show *The Moondog Rock & Roll House Party,* played early forms of Rock 'n' Roll and specifically called the music by that name, a phrase he was previously familiar with from Race Records and songs such as *Rock and Rolling Mama* (1939) and *Rock and Roll* (there were three songs named this in the late 1940s).

Freed was encouraged to call this mix of music "Rock and Roll" by his sponsor, record store owner Leo Mintz, who was trying to boost sales on Race Records by getting white shoppers to buy them. Race Records weren't very popular at the time among white people, but by re-branding the music "Rock and Roll", it quickly became extremely popular among teenagers of all ethnicities.

BONUS FACT

A similar brand of music to Rock 'n' Roll was "Rockabilly," which was a style of music that was a cross between Country, Rhythm, and Blues (as was Rock and Roll), but leaned more heavily on the Country side of things, instead of the Rhythm and Blues side, and was played primarily by white musicians. The term itself is a portmanteau of rock (from "Rock and Roll") and "hillbilly." Popular Rockabilly artists included Elvis Presley, Buddy Holly, Jerry Lee Lewis, and Johnny Cash.

Classic-style "Race Records" (not mixed with Country music) at this same time were in the process of being re-branded to "Rhythm and Blues," thanks to famed music journalist and producer Jerry Wexler.

As for "Country music," this was originally called "Hillbilly music," but in the 1940s, Ernest Tubb helped re-brand this type of music. Tubb stated, "Hillbilly, that's what the press use to call it, 'Hillbilly music.' Now, I always said, 'You can call me a hillbilly if you got a smile on your face.' We let the record companies know that they were producing Country music 'cause we all come from the country."

WHY DALMATIANS ARE THE TRADITIONAL DOG OF CHOICE AT FIRESTATIONS

One of the most effective fire-fighting tools in the mid-eighteenth century was the steam pumper -a machine that consisted of a boiler, which was able to use steam to force water out of hoses and onto a fire. The fire brigade's horse-drawn carriages, loaded with the machine, would be hitched up, and the vehicle would tear off down the road.

When fire fighters were racing off to fight the flames, they didn't have time to slow down for all the pedestrians using the road, which is where the Dalmatians came in.

Besides being known for forming strong bonds with horses, in the early 1700s, it was observed that Dalmatians were perfectly suited for traveling long distances. As stated by the Dalmatian Club of America, the English at this time felt that Dalmatians had the "strength, vitality, fortitude and size to keep running along under the carriage for hundreds of miles."

When the travelers rested for the night, the dogs were also useful for standing guard over the horses and the people's belongings. It soon became popular among English aristocrats to have Dalmatians run alongside their carriages, and the dogs even became something of a symbol of social status -the more you had running alongside your carriage, the wealthier you must be.

This brings us back to Dalmatians and the horse-drawn fire carriages. Because of the dogs' reputation and the long-standing practice of using them this way, they were the dog of choice for running along with fire carriages.

With their strength and stamina, they typically didn't have any trouble keeping up with the carriages even when the carriages were flying down the roads at high speeds. The Dalmatian would scare away anything that might spook the horses, as well as serve as the first "siren," with the Dalmatians' bark alerting pedestrians on the road that the fire brigade was on its way and to move off the street.

While the firemen unloaded their equipment and rushed off to put the fire out, their trusty Dalmatians would stay with the cart, keeping the horses calm and guarding the firemen's belongings.

Not only that, but once they were back at the fire house, the Dalmatians were often trained to sniff out and kill rats and other vermin.

When the much more efficient motorized fire trucks were created, there were no longer horses for Dalmatians to keep company and no need for them to run ahead of the trucks to alert people that the fire brigade was coming—there were sirens for that now. Their usefulness spent, Dalmatians might have vanished from fire stations altogether. Instead, they turned into fire station mascots, particularly popular when firefighters go around teaching kids about fire safety. Of course, at this point any dog could be used, and sometimes that's the case, but given the long-standing tradition of using Dalmatians, it seems likely they will remain the dog of choice at many fire stations for the foreseeable future.

BONUS FACT

A common myth is that Dalmatians were originally kept in fire houses because, unlike other breeds, the loud sound of the sirens won't hurt their ears. While it is true that Dalmatians are predisposed to deafness (only about 70% have normal hearing), they were originally around partially to function as a siren, as stated, so their hearing wasn't really a factor.

WHY "HANK" IS SHORT FOR "HENRY"

This is thought to be thanks to the one time popular suffix "-kin," which is also how "Jack" originally derived from the name "John." Specifically, the suffix "-kin," simply indicated "little," so Robin Hood's "Little John" would have been aptly named "Jockin," which later gave rise to "Jenkin," then "Jakin," and then "Jack," with the former forms literally meaning "Little John".

Similarly, we have "Little Henry" becoming "Henkin," which later gave rise to "Hankin," which was then shortened to just "Hank."

BONUS FACT

Another interesting nickname derivation is how we got "Dick" from "Richard." This is another one of those "knee bone connected to the thigh bone" type progressions. Due to people having to write everything by hand, shortened versions of Richard were common, such as 'Ric' or 'Rich'. This in turn gave rise to nicknames like 'Richie', 'Rick', and 'Ricket', among others. People also used to like to use rhyming names. Thus, someone who was nicknamed Rich might further be nicknamed Hitch. Thus, Richard -> Ric -> Rick gave rise to nicknames like Dick and Hick around the early 13th century.

WHY WE SAY "O'CLOCK"

The practice of saying "o'clock" is simply a remnant of simpler times when clocks weren't very prevalent and people told time by a variety of means, depending on where they were and what references were available.

Generally, of course, the Sun was used as a reference point, with solar time being slightly different than clock time. Clocks divide the time evenly, whereas, by solar time, hour lengths vary somewhat based on a variety of factors, like what season it is.

Thus, to distinguish the fact that one was referencing a clock's time, rather than something like a sundial, as early as the fourteenth century one would say something like, "It is six of the clock," which later got slurred down to "six o'clock" sometime around the sixteenth or seventeenth centuries. In those centuries, it was also somewhat common to just drop the "o'" altogether and just say something like "six clock."

Using the form of "o'clock" particularly increased in popularity around the eighteenth century when it became common to do a similar slurring in the names of many things such as "Will-o'-the wisp" from "Will of the wisp" (stemming from a legend of an evil blacksmith named Will Smith, with "wisp" meaning "torch") and "Jack-o'-lantern" from "Jack of the lantern" (which originally just meant "man of the lantern" with "Jack," at the time, being the generic "any man" name. Later, either this or the Irish legend of "Stingy Jack" got this name transferred to referring to carved pumpkins with lit candles inside).

While today with clocks being ubiquitous and few people, if anybody, telling direct time by the Sun, it isn't necessary in most cases to specify we are referencing time from clocks, but the practice of saying "o'clock" has stuck around anyway.

BONUS FACT

The word "clock" is thought to have originally derived from the Medieval Latin "clocca," meaning "bell," referencing the ringing of the bells on early town clocks, which would let everyone in a community know what time it was.

WHY BATHING WAS UNCOMMON IN MEDIEVAL EUROPE

Before the Middle Ages, public baths were very common, as was the general public regularly taking time to bathe, in one way or another. Even during the fourth and fifth centuries, Christian authorities allowed people to bathe for cleanliness and health, but they condemned attendance to public-bath houses for pleasure and condemned women going to bath-houses that had mixed facilities. Over time, more and more restrictions appeared. Eventually, Christians were prohibited from bathing naked and the church began to disallow an "excessive" indulgence in the habit of bathing. This culminated in the Medieval church authorities proclaiming that public bathing led to immorality, promiscuous sex, and diseases.

This latter "disease" point was very common; it was believed in many parts of Europe that water could carry disease into the body through the pores in the skin. According to one medical treaty of the sixteenth century, "Water baths warm the body, but weaken the organism and widen pores. That's why they can be dangerous and cause different diseases, even death."

It wasn't just diseases from the water itself they were worried about. They also felt that with the pores widened after a bath that this resulted in infections of the air having easier access to the body. Hence, bathing became connected with the spread of diseases, not just immorality.

For most lower-class citizens, particularly men, the threat of diseases resulted in them completely forgoing bathing. During this time, people tended to restrict their hygienic arrangements to just washing hands, parts of the face, and rinsing their mouths. Washing one's entire face was thought to be dangerous as it was believed to cause catarrh (inflammation of the mucous membranes in the airways or cavities of the body) and weaken the eyesight, so even this face washing was infrequent.

On the other hand, rather than completely forgo bathing, members of the upper classes tended to cut their full body bathing habits to around a few times per year, striking a balance between the risk of acquiring a disease from the bath vs. body stench.

This wasn't always the case though. As one Russian ambassador to France noted, "His Majesty [Louis XIV] stunk like a wild animal." Russians were not so finicky about bathing and tended to bathe fairly regularly, relatively speaking, generally at least once a month. Because of this, they were considered perverts by many Europeans. King Louis XIV's stench came from the fact that his physicians advised him to bathe as infrequently as possible to maintain good health. He also stated he found the act of bathing disturbing. Because of this, he is said to have only bathed twice in his lifetime. Another in this "gruesome two-some" class among the aristocracy was Queen Isabel I of Spain who once confessed that she had taken a bath only twice in her lifetime, when she was first born and when she got married.

To get around the water/disease and sinful nature of bathing, many aristocrats during the Middle Ages replaced bathing with scented rags to rub the body with and heavy use of perfumes to mask their stench. Men wore small bags with fragrant herbs between the shirt and waistcoat, while women used fragrant powders.

Amazingly, this complete lack of personal hygiene in most of Europe lingered until around the md-nineteenth century.

BONUS FACT

If most of the entire populace smelling rancid wasn't enough, during Medieval times in Europe, the streets of cities tended to be coated in feces and urine, thanks to people tossing the contents of their chamber pots into the streets. As one sixteenth century nobleman noted, "the streets resembled a fetid stream of turbid water." He also noted that he had to keep a scented handkerchief held under his nose in order to keep from vomiting when walking the streets. If that wasn't enough, butchers slaughtered animals in the streets and would leave the unusable bits and blood right on the ground. One can only imagine how people survived the stench on Sun-baked summer days.

WHY TUBERCULOSIS WAS CALLED "CONSUMPTION"

Originally, of course, nobody knew what caused the various forms of tuberculosis, and they certainly didn't understand it was caused by what would eventually be called tubercle bacillus (usually the offending microbes are specifically Mycobacterium tuberculosis). The word "tuberculosis" was coined by Johann Lukas Schönle in 1839, from the Latin "tuberculum," meaning "small, swelling bump or pimple." However, it wouldn't be until 1882 when Dr. Robert Koch discovered the tubercle bacillus, for which he won a Nobel Prize in 1905, that the name "tuberculosis" began being exclusively used to refer to the disease formerly popularly known as consumption.

Of course, the microbes that cause the disease have been around for at least 15,000-20,000 years with known human deaths being caused by the bacteria dating back at least as far as 5,000 years ago, so the current name is an extremely recent moniker relative to how long the disease has been around.

The much older name originally came from the ancient Greeks who called the disease something meaning "consumption," "phthisis," specifically referring to pulmonary tuberculosis, with the earliest references to this being in 460 BC.

The "father of Western medicine," Hippocrates, estimated that phthisis was the most widespread disease of his age. He further told his students that they shouldn't attempt to treat patients in the last stages of phthisis, as they were sure to die and it would ruin his protégés' reputation as healers if they made a practice of attempting to heal such individuals.

Tuberculosis wasn't just found across the pond either, but it is known to have been present in the Americas as early as 100 AD.

So why was "phthisis" aka "consumption" chosen for the name? It was because the disease seemed to consume the individual, with their weight drastically dropping as the disease progressed.

BONUS FACT

While many today in developed countries consider tuberculosis to be a thing of the past, this isn't the case at all. There are over eight million new cases of people contracting TB every year in the world, with about two million people per year dying from the disease.

WHY SOME COINS HAVE RIDGES

Putting ridges on some coins in America got its start back in the 1700s. At this time, coins were actually made of materials that were worth what the coin was worth. For example, a half dollar silver coin contained fifty cents worth of silver. Likewise, a $10 gold coin contained $10 worth of gold.

As a consequence of this, people started to shave off bits of these coins around the edges; so then a $10 gold piece only contained, say, $9.50 worth of gold. The payoff came from that if they were very careful when they shaved the coins, it was difficult to tell that anything had been shaved off, so they could still generally get their $10 worth out of the now $9.50 piece. Over time, they'd collect the shavings and when they had a large enough amount, they'd go sell them.

Eventually, the government decided to do something about this. One of the methods to combat this practice was to add ridges to these coins; something known as "reeding" the coins. With the ridges on the edges, it became significantly more difficult to shave anything off the coins without detection. The government chose not to do this with smaller valued coins that came out later (pennies and nickels), because the metals these coins contained weren't valuable enough for shaving them to be worth the effort.

So that was then, why do they still do it today when the coins are no longer made of valuable metals? Initially, it was supposedly easier and cheaper than modifying the existing machinery. Today, however, it is to help the visually impaired to more easily distinguish between coins of a somewhat similar size like a penny and a dime. This is something unfortunately not done with today's American paper money, which is indistinguishable to blind people without resorting to tricks like folding them certain ways for different bills or Braille money stampers. The blind still need someone to tell them what the bill is in the first place when they receive it, so they can do whatever they do to it to be able to distinguish it later on their own. Although, supposedly the government is working on this problem with one of the most popular suggested solutions being to adopt the new Canadian system of imprinting the bills with Braille.

WHY PAPER CUTS HURT SO MUCH

The generally accepted reason paper cuts are so painful primarily lies in the fact that you usually get them on your fingers, particularly your fingertips. Fingertips and hands have significantly more nociceptors (nerve fibers) per square millimeter than most of the rest of your body, such as your legs, arms, stomach area, etc. This ends up making cuts on your fingertips feel significantly more painful than cuts elsewhere, even when they are produced by paper or similar objects.

That's fine for the reason why paper cuts hurt so much more than other cuts on the rest of the body, but why do paper cuts seem to hurt more than other types of cuts on the hand? This is thought to be because the edges of paper are very dull and flexible, compared to knives and other such sharp objects. Because of this, when the paper cuts your flesh, it does a lot more microscopic damage as it rips through your skin. Think of it like a dull knife that you are trying to use to cut into a steak. You have to saw at it more than you would with a sharp knife and, in the end, the cut you made is a lot more mutilated than a cut with a very sharp knife. With paper cuts, you can't see this with the naked eye, but the same type of thing is happening.

Not only is there more microscopic damage, but this damage is also very shallow on the skin. This will further increase the pain because some of the most sensitive nerves in your skin, which have very low thresholds to trigger, are near the surface. This will result in a much sharper and distinct pain than if the cut had been deeper and caused the same type of damage to nerves deep in your flesh, which would send back signals to the brain more akin to a throbbing sensation when they are activated.

Further, the paper cut, being a very shallow wound, will also tend to hurt longer because it won't bleed much and sometimes not at all. This leaves the nerves open to the air and other irritants, so they will continue to be in an activated state for much longer than more significant cuts.

WHY THE SAME SIDE OF THE MOON ALWAYS FACES THE EARTH

One Moon "day" is approximately 29 1/2 Earth days. This rotation coincides with its orbit around the Earth so that we only see about 59% of the surface of the Moon. When the Moon first formed, its rotational speed and orbit were very different than they are now. Over time, the Earth's gravitational field gradually slowed the Moon's rotation until the orbital period and the rotational speed stabilized, making one side of the Moon always face the Earth.

How does this work? Simply put -tidal friction. For a slightly less simple explanation, we'll have to put our science caps on. But stick with it; it's fascinating. I promise.

To start, think of how the Moon causes major tides on the Earth due to the Moon pulling at the Earth via its gravitational field. The Earth has this same effect on the Moon and, being 81.28 times more massive, the effect is much more powerful.

So, as the mass of the Moon is attempting to go one way (in a straight line), the Earth is simultaneously pulling it another way (towards the Earth). Further, the effect of the Earth's gravitational field is stronger on the side of the Moon closest to the Earth than on the far side (and the same with the Moon's gravitational field's effect on the different parts of the surface of the Earth).

This combination essentially stretches the Earth and Moon, creating tidal bulges on both celestial bodies. This occurs on both sides of each, with the bulge on the sides closest together from gravity and on the sides farthest away from inertia. In the latter case, the matter is less affected by the gravitational force with inertia dominating in this case. To put it another way, the matter is trying to move in a straight line away from the Earth and the gravitational forces here aren't as strongly able to overcome this, which creates the bulge on that side.

So back before the Moon was tidally locked with the Earth, the bulge on the side of the Moon nearest to Earth ended up slightly leading thanks to friction and the fact that the Moon rotated faster than its orbital period around the Earth. So with this slightly leading bulge being offset from the line of gravitational pull between the Moon and Earth, this created a torque, which overtime resulted in the Moon's rotation slowing until it became tidally locked with the Earth; thus, only one side faces the Earth. (Note: the bulge on the far side of the Moon had the opposite effect, but the bulge closest to the Earth dominated the interaction.)

You'll note, though, that I said we actually get to see about 59% of the surface of the Moon from Earth, not 50%. The discrepancy comes from the fact that the Moon's orbit around the Earth isn't perfectly circular, more of an ellipse. As the Moon's distance from the Earth increases and decreases, its angular speed changes, while its rotational speed stays the same. The result is that we get to see an extra 9% of its surface than we would if it had a perfectly circular orbit.

The other side of this, as you may have guessed, is that the Moon has the same effect on the Earth and is gradually slowing the Earth's rotation in the exact same way the Moon became tidally locked with the Earth. Further, as the Moon slows the Earth's rotation, a small portion of the Earth's rotational momentum gets transferred to the Moon's orbital momentum, with the result being that the average radius of the Moon's orbit increases at about 3.8 centimeters per year with the current continental positions and barring major geological events. (Contrary to what you'll often read, the Moon isn't getting all the energy here, most of it is being converted to heat via friction, with only an estimated 3% of the energy in the interaction being "stolen" by the Moon.)

Thus, the distance between the Moon and the Earth changes gradually and is more or less in step with the rotational period change. It should be noted, though, that it's not a constant change as things like major earthquakes, glacial changes, continental drift, and other such geological events play a role here, which is why leap seconds aren't added at regular intervals, but only when needed. But the overall effect is that over time, the Moon is getting farther and farther away from the Earth every year, while the Earth's rotation is slowing down.

In theory, at some point tens of billions of years from now (with the exact timeframe being extremely difficult to nail down due to so many unknowable factors) the same side of the Earth will always face the Moon, with the Earth only rotating once per lunar cycle, which at that point most estimates indicate should be about 47 current Earth days long.

"In theory"... but this will likely never happen. Why? In about 1 to 2 billion years or so, the Sun's brightness will have increased sufficiently to vaporize all water on the surface of the Earth, getting rid of the ocean tides altogether, which is a huge factor in this interaction. However, there still would be some bulging of the Earth's crust to continue the process to a much lesser extent.

In 5 to 6 billion years, the Sun will be around the peak of its Red Giant phase, and according to the latest models, even with the Sun losing quite a bit of mass during this process, thus making the Earth's orbit farther out, the Sun should just barely consume the Earth and Moon many billions of years before such a dual tidal lock can occur.

Bottom line, at some point in the next billion years or so, humans will need to either find another home, or figure out how to manually move our current one to a farther out orbit, keeping Earth in the habitable zone of our solar system.

BONUS FACT

There is technically no true "dark side" of the Moon. As noted, the Moon is still rotating and, despite the fact that we don't see it, the opposite side from our perspective still gets sunlight during that side's "day". In fact, the only time the "dark side" of the Moon is truly totally dark is when we are seeing a full Moon.

WHY "COLONEL" IS PRONOUNCED "KERNEL"

Believe it or not, "colonel" was pronounced more or less the way it originally looked when it was introduced to English. The spelling changed over time to "colonel", while the pronunciation stayed the same as it was before.

"Colonel" ultimately derives from the Latin "columna," meaning "pillar." This gave rise to the Old Italian "compagna colonnella," meaning "little-column company." This, in turn, gave us the rank of "colonnello" -the leader of a column.

Other nations adopted this ranking giving us the Middle French "Coronel." This was pronounced pretty much like it looks at first, then later slurred down to "Kernel" by the English, but using the same spelling.

However, starting with the French around the 1540s, the spelling was changed back closer to the Italian spelling, which gave us "Colonel" in French.

Within a few decades, the English also followed suit and by the mid-seventeenth century, "colonel" was the most common way to spell the word in English. At that time, the common pronunciation was mixed between the older "kernel" and the new "colonel," with the former winning out in the end, despite the way it's spelled.

WHY THREE STRIKES IN A ROW IN BOWLING IS CALLED A "TURKEY"

This is thought to have its origins in bowling tournament prizes. Late eighteenth and early nineteenth century prizes given out during these tournaments were often food items, such as a basket filled with various grocery items, a large ham, or the like. Particularly around Thanksgiving in the United States, turkeys became common prizes. At some point (no one knows the exact first instance), one tournament decided to give away a turkey to people who managed to bowl three strikes in a row. This practice spread and eventually embedded itself in common bowling vernacular, long after giving away actual turkeys stopped.

You might wonder how those individuals running tournaments managed to make any money at all when they were giving away a turkey every time someone bowled three strikes in a row, let alone prizes for other accomplishments. After all, even complete amateurs can achieve that feat on occasion, and those who are skilled can do it with some regularity.

But in the late eighteenth and early nineteenth centuries, bowling three strikes in a row was extremely hard to do owing to the fact that they didn't have nearly the refined, pristine lanes we're used to today. Further, the pins were setup by hand, sometimes in a not quite uniform fashion; bowling balls tended not to be well balanced; and people running the tournaments would often use tricks to make the pins harder to knock down, such as adding weight in the bottoms of the pins. So bowling three strikes in a row was exceptionally hard to do, even for those who were highly skilled.

With it being somewhat more common to hit three strikes or more in a row today, new names have been developed to account for the strike-bloat, though usage of these terms isn't nearly as widespread as with a "Turkey."

That being said, relatively common terms include:
- Four consecutive strikes: Hambone
- Six consecutive strikes: Wild Turkey
- Nine consecutive strikes: Golden Turkey
- A Perfect Game, all strikes from start to finish: Dinosaur

(supposedly originally because it's "non-existent like a dinosaur", though in fact it has been done several times, such as by Grazio Castellano who was the first to bowl a perfect game on live television on October 4, 1953.)

In general, if you can't remember these names and you want to sound like you know what you're talking about, you can simply call them a "four bagger," "five bagger," etc. for four and five strikes in a row and beyond.

WHY TURKEYS ARE CALLED "TURKEYS"

In the sixteenth century, when North American turkeys were first introduced en masse to Europe, there was another bird that was popularly imported throughout Europe and, most relevant to this topic, England, called a guinea fowl. This guinea fowl was imported from Madagascar via the Ottoman Empire. The merchants who imported the guinea fowl were thus known as "turkey merchants." The guinea fowl eventually were popularly referred to as "turkey fowl," similar to how other product imported through the Ottoman Empire acquired their names, such as "turkey corn," "turkey wheat," etc.

The North American turkey was first introduced to Spain in the very early sixteenth century and popularly introduced to all of Europe shortly thereafter. The animal was thought by many to be a species of the type of guinea fowl that was imported via the Ottoman Empire and thus, began also being called a "turkey fowl" in English, with this eventually being shortened to just "turkey."

BONUS FACT

Due to white meat being the most popular part of a turkey, domestic turkeys have been bred to have huge breasts. So much so that modern-day domesticated turkeys are no longer typically able to mate, due to the breasts getting in the way of the male mounting the female. As such, most hatcheries use artificial insemination to fertilize the eggs of the domestic turkey.

WHY PISTACHIOS USED TO BE DYED RED

Historically, most pistachios in the United States were imported from the Middle East. The problem was that when they arrived, they tended to have numerous blemishes on the shells, particularly stains left over from the harvesting methods employed in the Middle East. These stains weren't good for marketing purposes. To get around this, importers devised an idea to not only mask the blemishes, but also to help draw the eye to the pistachios, namely, dying them red.

This all began to change in the 1970s when pistachios started to be grown in the U.S. commercially. Today, the vast majority (upwards of 98%) of pistachios sold in the United States are grown and processed in California with much better harvesting and processing facilities than decades before in the Middle East. These improved facilities result in fewer blemishes and stains appearing on the pistachios, so there is less need to dye them, which is one of the reasons the practice is dying out.

BONUS FACT

Like the cashew, pistachios are a member of the Anacardiaceae family, meaning they, too, naturally contain the chemical urushiol that makes poison ivy and others in the family so irritating. In the pistachio's case, the primary concentration of urushiol is in the pistachio itself.

WHY TOOTHPASTE MAKES THINGS LIKE ORANGE JUICE TASTE SO AWFUL

You may think it might be the common mint flavor of toothpaste clashing with other flavors, but in the case of orange juice and many other things, this isn't actually what's going on. The culprit here is thought to be two compounds almost universally added to toothpastes -sodium lauryl sulfate and sodium lauryl ether sulfate, which are anionic surfactants, meaning they lower the surface tension of water.

Why is that desirable in toothpaste? Because it works as something of a detergent, and makes the toothpaste foam to help it spread around inside your mouth easier. Besides any cleaning effect, this has the by-product of making you feel like the toothpaste is doing something, which toothpaste manufacturers have found to be a great way to get people to buy more of their toothpaste.

Mint is added to toothpaste for this same reason, as it leaves your mouth feeling cool, clean, and fresh, particularly if it's well distributed throughout your mouth. As Tracy Sinclair, one-time brand manager at Oral-B stated in the book *The Power of Habit*, "Consumers need some kind of signal that a product is working. We can make toothpaste taste like anything — blueberries, green tea — and as long as it has a cool tingle, people feel like their mouth is clean. The tingling doesn't make the toothpaste work any better. It just convinces people it's doing the job."

(Interestingly enough, besides any real cleaning effect, sodium lauryl sulfate is added to shampoo for similar marketing reasons, as people perceive that foaming shampoo works better than non-foaming, whether a particular brand's foaming shampoo actually cleans better than some other non-foaming shampoo or not.)

Back to your taste-buds -the sodium lauryl sulfate interacts with your sweet taste receptors, making them less sensitive, and thus dulling the sweet flavor. In addition to that, it also destroys phospholipids in your mouth, which are compounds that have the same type of effect sodium lauryl sulfate has on sweet taste buds, except the phospholipids dampen your bitter taste buds.

34

The net effect is that your sweet taste buds are dampened while your bitter taste buds become more sensitive. So when you drink something like orange juice, which normally has an overpowering sweet taste that masks an underlying bitter taste, it is going to taste drastically different -in this case extremely bitter.

So if for some reason your morning routine includes brushing your teeth before eating, you can simply find toothpaste that is free of sodium lauryl sulfate, and sodium lauryl ether sulfate and the food you eat directly after shouldn't taste awful, unless you're bad at cooking, of course.

BONUS FACT

Sodium lauryl sulfate has been shown to act as a shark repellent. There is also evidence that it is effective as a microbicide when spread on your skin, particularly effective in helping to prevent infection from viruses like Herpes simplex and HIV, which are non-enveloped viruses.

WHY WE HAVE A SEVEN-DAY WEEK

Two of the earliest known civilizations to use a seven-day week were the Babylonians and the Jews. The Babylonians marked time with lunar months, and it is thought by many scholars that this is why they chose a seven-day week (though direct evidence of lunar months being why they declared a seven-day week is scant).

That being said, each lunar month was made up of several different cycles—on the first day, the first visible crescent appeared; on approximately the seventh day, the waxing half-Moon could be seen; on approximately the fourteenth, the full Moon; on approximately the twenty-first, the waning half-Moon; and on approximately the twenty-eighth, the last visible crescent. As you can see, each notable cycle is made up of about seven days, hence, the seven-day week.

You'll notice I used the word "approximate" a lot in there. This is because the Moon phases don't line up perfectly with this schedule. As such, as far back as the sixth century BC (which incidentally is also around the time the Jews were captives in Babylon), the Babylonians would sometimes have three seven-day weeks, followed by an eight to nine day week, presumably to re-synchronize the start and end of the weeks to match the phases of the Moon.

In their normal seven-day week, the Babylonians held the seventh day of each week as holy, much like the Jews did and still do. However, the Babylonians also held the day to be unlucky. Thus, similar to the Jews (but for a different reason, the unluckiness of the day), the seventh day had restrictions on certain activities to avoid dire consequences from the inherit unluckiness of the day. The final "seventh day" of the month for the Babylonians was a day of rest and worship.

The ancient Romans, during the Republic, did not use a seven-day week but rather went with eight days. One "eighth day" of every week was set aside as a shopping day where people would buy and sell things, particularly buying food supplies for the following week.

Rather than labeling the days of the week with actual names, at this time the Romans labeled them with letters, A-H. You might think from this that the "H" was always the shopping day, but this isn't correct. You see, the calendar year did not divide evenly by eight. Thus, the day of the week that was the day to go shopping changed every year, but they still often referred to a particular day based on its proximity to the shopping day.

For reasons not entirely clear, within a century after the introduction of the Julian Calendar in 46 BC, the eight-day week started to diminish in popularity in favor of the seven-day week. The full switch was not sudden, happening over centuries. For a time, as the seven-day week grew in popularity, both the seven and eight-day weeks were used in Rome simultaneously. Finally, after the popularity of the eight-day week diminished almost completely, Constantine, the first Christian Roman Emperor, made the seven-day week official in AD 321. Due to the influence of both Rome and Christianity, this has stuck in most regions of the world ever since.

BONUS FACT

For a very brief time in France and the USSR, the seven-day week was abandoned. The French abandoned the seven-day week in favor of a ten-day week beginning in 1793 thanks to the French Republican Calendar developed in France at that time. This was abandoned nine years later when the Roman Catholic Church was re-established in France. The official switch back to the seven-day week happened on April 18, 1802, Easter Sunday.

Starting in 1929, the USSR abandoned the seven-day week in favor of at first a five-day week, then a six-day week. This was abandoned and the seven-day week was re-established in 1940.

WHY A TYPICAL WORKDAY IS EIGHT HOURS LONG

During the Industrial Revolution, companies attempted to maximize the output of their factories by keeping them running as many hours as possible, typically implementing a "Sun up to Sun down" workday. Wages were also extremely low, so employees often needed to work these long shifts just to get by financially. The typical workday at this time lasted anywhere from 10-18 hours per day, six days a week. This all began to change in the nineteenth century.

The first person to suggest an eight-hour workday for everyone was a British man by the name of Robert Owen, who was also one of the founders of socialism. Owen felt that a day should be divided into thirds, with workers getting equal time to themselves and to sleep as they do for work. Thus, in 1817, he began campaigning for an eight-hour working day for all workers, coining the slogan, "Eight hours labour, eight hours recreation, eight hours rest." Unfortunately, this did not catch on for some time, though throughout the nineteenth century a series of Factories Acts were passed that steadily improved working conditions and reduced work hours for factory workers. For instance, The Factories Act of 1847 stipulated that women and children were to be granted a ten hour workday, thus only having to work 60 hours per week, as opposed to the former amount which in many cases was over 100 hours per week.

The eight-hour workday cause was taken up once again in Britain, in 1884, by Tom Mann who was part of the Social Democratic Federation. Mann subsequently formed an "Eight Hour League" whose sole goal was to get the eight-hour workday established. Their biggest victory came when they managed to convince the Trades Union Congress, which represented the majority of unions in Britain (and does so even to this day), to establish the eight-hour workday as one of their primary goals, which they subsequently began to work towards.

The push for a shorter workday began earlier in the United States, in 1791, with workers in Philadelphia striking for a ten-hour total workday that would include two hours for meals. By the 1830s, support for eight-hour workdays was shared among the majority of the working-class people in the United States, but still failed to find support among business owners. Over the next few decades, workers continued to hold strikes demanding shorter working hours and gradually things improved.

Momentum for the cause particularly picked up with several "Eight Hour Leagues" forming in the United States, as Mann had formed in Britain around this same time. In 1884, the Federation of Organized Trades and Labor Unions declared that May 1, 1886 would be the first day that an eight-hour workday would be made mandatory. This, of course, was neither backed by any federal mandate nor the businesses themselves, and it relied on workers striking and raising a general ruckus to drive the point home. When May 1, 1886 arrived, the first ever May Day Parade was held with 350,000 workers walking off their jobs protesting for the eight-hour workday.

Progress was still slow though, and it wasn't until 1905 that industries began implementing the eight-hour workday on their own accord. One of the first businesses to implement this was the Ford Motor Company, in 1914, which not only cut the standard workday to eight hours, but also doubled their worker's pay per hour. To the shock of many, this resulted in Ford's overall output per workday increasing significantly, despite the fact that the company was using the same workers, who were now working fewer hours. This encouraged other companies to adopt the shorter, eight hour workday as a standard for their employees.

Finally, in 1937 the eight hour workday was standardized in the United States and regulated by the federal government according to the Fair Labor Standards Act. It stipulated that workers were not to work more than 44 hours per week and any hours over the 40 required of the workers were to be paid with overtime bonuses added to their normal pay rate.

BONUS FACT

Despite some groups in the United States, such as the Boston Ship Carpenters, managing to achieve an eight hour workday as early as 1842, the average work week in the United States in 1890 was around 90 to 100 hours per week for most building tradesmen, according to a survey done by the federal government at that time.

WHY GOLF BALLS HAVE DIMPLES

Somewhat counter intuitively, dimples in golf balls significantly decrease the drag on the golf ball as it flies through the air, compared to a smooth ball. Not only that, but the dimples also increase the lift somewhat. These two things combined can make the golf ball go as much as three times farther than the same ball without dimples.

The dimples on golf balls accomplish both of these things by creating turbulence in the layer of air around the golf ball, called the boundary layer. In simple terms, the dimples more or less scoop the air and direct it inwards towards the back of the golf ball. This effectively increases the net air pressure in the back of the ball, which reduces the drag by reducing the pressure pulling back at the ball from behind. This can reduce drag by as much as 50% over a smooth ball.

More technically, the streamline flow of air on a smooth ball separates fairly quickly from the ball as it passes over the surface of the golf ball. This ends up maximizing the size of the wake behind the golf ball, which maximizes the area of lower pressure, creating a large drag. With the dimpled golf balls, this streamline flow remains attached to the surface of the ball much longer, creating a smaller low-pressure region behind the ball, thereby significantly reducing the drag on the ball.

The dimples also create lift when there is significant backspin on the ball as it flies through the air. This is very similar to how the seams of a baseball create lift when there is backspin. In both cases, the backspin causes the air to move faster backwards on the top of the ball -with the golf ball via the dimples and with the baseball via the seams. This creates lower air pressure above the ball than below, which creates a small amount of lift. A similar effect can also be observed with baseballs and golf balls when a ball has a certain amount of side-spin. Except, in this case, instead of creating lift upwards, it will cause the ball to tail to one side or the other, depending on the direction of spin. This is why balls with this side-spin tend to travel in a sideways arc through the air.

You might be asking yourself, "Why don't they put dimples on planes, cars, and the like to reduce drag?" Primarily because creating turbulence in the boundary layer doesn't always reduce the net drag. It largely depends on the shape of the object and the speed at which it is traveling, among other things. For an object in the shape of a ball, where the primary drag is created by the wake, this ends up decreasing the net drag significantly. In more streamlined objects, such as an airplane wing, they create very little wake relative to the skin friction drag they experience. So the dimples wouldn't help much and, indeed, creating this turbulence would actually increase the streamline drag, which would drastically increase the skin friction while not helping much with the less significant drag caused by separation in the wake.

Now, as far as cars go, which tend to not be all that aerodynamically shaped relative to something like an airplane wing, it has been shown that creating a dimpled surface can decrease the overall drag somewhat on certain designs of cars. However, the difference in fuel efficiency is fairly marginal and hasn't, to date, been shown to be near significant enough to warrant sacrificing certain cosmetic aspects of the car by adding dimples.

BONUS FACT

Most golf balls have between 350 to 500 dimples, though the pattern, depth, and number vary significantly between different manufacturers.

WHY RED MEAT TURNS BROWN WHEN COOKED

This is thanks to a protein called myoglobin, which also is what makes raw red meat look red, not blood, as many people think. Myoglobin is a protein that stores oxygen in muscle cells, very similar to its cousin, hemoglobin, that stores oxygen in red blood cells. This oxygen store is necessary for muscles which need immediate oxygen for energy during continual usage.

So how does the myoglobin end up making the meat turn brown when cooked? This darkening effect is due to the oxidation state of the iron atoms in myoglobin. When the myoglobin is exposed to oxygen, before you cook the meat, the iron atom oxidation level is +2 and it is bound to a dioxygen molecule ($O2$), which makes the meat appear bright red. As you cook the meat, this iron atom loses an electron and goes to a +3 oxidation level. This process turns the meat brown.

White meat, on the other hand, doesn't turn dark brown like red meat because it has significantly less myoglobin in it. In fact, the myoglobin levels are actually one of the main factors that officially distinguish white meat from red meat.

BONUS FACT

Contrary to popular belief, "searing" meat does not in any way "seal the juices in." Water in seared meat evaporates at either the same rate or a higher rate, in some cases, than non-seared meat. What searing does do is play a role in browning, which can affect the flavor. But, in this case, the browning is caused by caramelization of sugars combined with a chemical reaction with amino acids and the sugars.

WHY AMISH MEN WEAR BEARDS BUT NOT MOUSTACHES

This tradition stems back to the early days of the Amish when wearing elaborate moustaches was common among those in the military. (In fact, this became so popular that from 1860 to 1916, British soldiers were actually required to have moustaches).

The Amish, being a pacifist group (not just in war, but also in all confrontation, which is why they prefer the term "non-resistance" to "pacifism"), didn't want to associate themselves with those who waged war, so they strictly forbade their members from growing moustaches. Today, few men in the Western world choose to grow moustaches, but this tradition remains among the Old Order Amish people, which number about 200,000 in North America.

While moustaches are not allowed, beards are practically a requirement among the Amish due to beards being common among men in the Bible. However, not all Amish men are traditionally allowed to grow beards. It isn't until an Amish man gets married that he will stop shaving his beard and allow it to grow out, with beards being a mark of an Amish male having become a man.

WHY THE TOILET IS COMMONLY KNOWN AS "THE CRAPPER"

It all started with U.S. soldiers stationed in England during WWI. The toilets in England at the time were predominately made by the company "Thomas Crapper & Co Ltd", with the company's name appearing on the toilets. The soldiers took to calling toilets "The Crapper" and brought that slang term for the toilet back with them to the United States.

If you're wondering, the word "crap" does not derive from "Crapper". While the origins of the word "crap" are not entirely known, it is known that it was commonly used in England to refer to rubbish or chaff, but fell out of use in the sixteenth century, long before Thomas Crapper and his company came along.

The term "crap" was still used somewhat in America though, originally coming over before the slang term died out in England, and it is thought that one of the reasons American soldiers seemed to universally take to calling the toilet "The Crapper" is that they found it funny with "crap" meaning something to the effect of "refuse" and that most of the cisterns and toilets in England were stamped with "T. Crapper & Co Ltd." It was ironical to them, though the joke was lost on the English who had long since stopped using the term "crap."

BONUS FACT

The founder of the company, Thomas Crapper (born around 1836 and died in 1910), was a famous plumber- at least as famous as plumbers can be. He was the official plumber of a few individuals of the royal family of the day and owned one of the larger plumbing companies in England.

WHY CARBONATED BEVERAGES ARE CALLED "SOFT DRINKS"

Today, the term "soft drink" is typically used for flavored carbonated beverages, but originally it was just any drink that didn't contain a significant amount of alcohol ("hard drink").

The push to have "soft drink" primarily refer to just sugary carbonated beverages is thanks to a concerted effort by carbonated beverage makers. Flavored carbonated beverage makers were having a hard time creating national advertisements due to the fact that what people call their product varies from place to place. For instance, in parts of the United States and Canada, flavored carbonated beverages are referred to as "pop"; in other parts "soda"; in yet other parts "coke"; and there are a variety of other names commonly used as well. If we go international with the advertisements, in England these drinks are called "fizzy drinks"; in Ireland sometimes "minerals."

To account for the fact that they can't refer to their product in the generic sense on national advertisements because of these varied terms, these manufactures chose the term "soft drink" to be more or less a universal term for flavored carbonated beverages. Thanks to the subsequent advertising campaigns that followed featuring this, today "soft drink" almost exclusively refers to these beverages, rather than any non-alcoholic drink as before.

BONUS FACT

The first known reference of the term "pop," as referring to a beverage, was in 1812 in a letter written by English poet Robert Southey. In this letter, he also explains the term's origin: "Called on A. Harrison and found he was at Carlisle, but that we were expected to supper; excused ourselves on the necessity of eating at the inn; supped there upon trout and roast foul, drank some most admirable cyder, and a new manufactory of a nectar, between soda-water and ginger-beer, and called pop, because 'pop goes the cork' when it is drawn, and pop you would go off too, if you drank too much of it."

WHY WE DIVIDE THE DAY INTO SECONDS, MINUTES, AND HOURS

Today the most widely used numerical system is a base 10 system (decimal). This seems appropriate given we all have 10 fingers and toes, so grade-schoolers (and myself, after a few beers) can do math easily! Unfortunately for us, the pre-Dewey Decimal civilizations either never tried to count their sheep drunk, or just plain hated their kids because they all seemed to use other more complicated systems like a base 12 (duodecimal) or base 60 (sexagesimal).

The first society credited with separating the day out into smaller parts was the Egyptians. They divided a day into two twelve-hour sections: night and day. The clock they used to measure time was the sundial. The first sundials were just stakes in the ground and you knew what time it was by the length and direction of the Sun's shadow. Advances in technology, namely a t-shaped bar placed into the ground, allowed them to more accurately measure the day in 12 distinct parts.

The drawback to this early clock was that at night there was no real way to measure time. Egyptians, like us, still needed to measure time after dark. After all, how else would we know when the bars close? So their early astronomers observed a set of 36 stars, 18 of which they used to mark the passage of time after the Sun was down. Six of them would be used to mark the 3 hours of twilight on either side of the night and twelve then would be used to divide up the darkness into 12 equal parts. Later on, somewhere between 1550 and 1070 BC, this system was simplified to just use a set of 24 stars, 12 of which were used to mark the passage of time.

There were many other methods, in ancient times, for measuring the passage of time after dark. The most accurately known clock was a water clock, called a clepsydra. Dating back to approximately 1400-1500 BC, this device was able to mark the passage of time during various months, despite the seasons. It used a slanting interior surface that was inscribed with scales that allowed for a decrease in water pressure as the water flowed out of a hole at the bottom of the vessel.

Whatever method of tracking time used, the idea of dividing up time into 24 hour cycles was now firmly entrenched.

Interestingly enough, it wasn't until about 150 BC that the Greek astronomer Hipparchus suggested that a fixed interval for each hour was needed. He proposed dividing up the day into 24 equinoctial hours observed on equinox days. That said, it wasn't until about the fourteenth century, when mechanical clocks were commonplace, that a fixed length for an hour became widely accepted.

Hipparchus and other astronomers used astronomical techniques they borrowed from the Babylonians who made calculations using a base 60 system. It's unknown why the Babylonians, who inherited it from the Sumerians, originally chose to use 60 as a base for a calculation system. However, it is extremely convenient for expressing fractions of time using 10, 12, 15, 20 and 30.

Using this base 60 system as a means of dividing up the hour was born from the idea of devising a geographical system to mark the Earth's geometry. The Greek astronomer Eratosthenes, who lived between 276 and 194 B.C., used this sexagesimal system to divide a circle into 60 parts. These lines of latitude were horizontal and ran through well-known places on the Earth at the time. Later, Hipparchus devised longitudinal lines that encompassed 360 degrees. Even later, the astronomer Claudius Ptolemy expanded on Hipparchus' work and divided each of the 360 degrees of latitude and longitude into 60 equal parts. These parts were further subdivided into 60 smaller parts. He called the first division "partes minutae primae," or first minute. The subdivided smaller parts he called "partes minutae secundae," or second minute, which became known as the second.

BONUS FACT

Because the second is based on the number of times the cesium atom transitions between the two hyperfine levels of its ground state compared to ephemeris time, and the fact that the earth's rotation is slowing down, it becomes necessary to add periodic "leap seconds" into the atomic timescale to keep the two within one second of each other.

WHY SALT ENHANCES FLAVOR

This is partially due to the fact that "saltiness" is one of the five primary basic tastes the human tongue can detect. Those five tastes being: salt, bitter, sweet, sour, and umami (if you're not familiar with this one, it is from glutamic acid, which is found in many foods, particularly some meats, and is the basis of the flavor enhancer monosodium glutamate, also known as MSG).

The extra salt has other effects as well though, outside of simply making things more salty. Particularly, adding salt to foods helps certain molecules in those foods more easily release into the air, thus helping the aroma of the food, which is important in our perception of taste.

Adding a bit of salt won't just increase your salty taste perception, but it will also suppress your bitter taste perception in any given food (which is why it is often sprinkled on grape fruit, for instance, before eating).

Finally, adding salt to sweet or sour things, while not shown to suppress sweet or sour flavors like it does with bitter flavors, will help balance the taste a bit by making the perceived flavor, for instance of sugary candies or lemons, less one-dimensional.

BONUS FACT

The word "salad" comes from the ancient Roman practice of salting leaf vegetables; "salad" literally means "salted."

WHY LEAD USED TO BE ADDED TO GASOLINE

"Tetraethyl lead" was used in early model cars to help reduce engine knocking, boost octane ratings, and help with wear and tear on valve seats within the motor. Due to concerns over air pollution and health risks, this type of gas was slowly phased out starting in the late 1970s and banned altogether in all on-road vehicles in the United States in 1995.

For a more detailed explanation of why lead used to be added to gasoline, it's necessary to understand a little bit more about gasoline and what properties make it a good combustion material in car engines. Gasoline is a product of crude oil that is made of carbon atoms joined together into carbon chains. The different length of the chains creates different fuels. For example, methane has one carbon atom, propane has three, and octane has eight carbon atoms chained together. These chains have characteristics that behave differently under various circumstances; characteristics like boiling point and ignition temperature, for instance, can vary greatly between them. As fuel is compressed in a motor's cylinder, it heats up. Should the fuel reach its ignition temperature during compression, it will auto-ignite at the wrong time. This causes loss of power and damage to the engine. Fuels such as heptane (which has seven carbon atoms chained together) can ignite under very little compression. Octane, however, tends to handle compression extremely well.

The higher the compression in the cylinders a car's motor can produce, the greater the power it can get out of each stroke of the piston. This makes it necessary to have fuels that can handle higher compression without auto-igniting. The higher the octane rating, the more compression the fuel can handle. An octane rating of 87 means the fuel is a mixture of 87% octane and 13 percent heptane, or any mixture of fuels or additives that have the same performance of 87/13.

In 1919, Dayton Metal Products Co. merged with General Motors. They formed a research division that set out to solve two problems: the need for high compression engines and the insufficient supply of fuel that would run them. On December 9,

1921, chemists led by Charles F. Kettering and his assistants, Thomas Midgley and T.A. Boyd added Tetraethyl lead to the fuel in a laboratory engine. The ever present knock, caused by auto-ignition of fuel being compressed past its ignition temperature, was completely silenced. Most all automobiles at the time were subject to this engine knock so the research team was overjoyed. Over time, other manufacturers found that by adding lead to fuel they could significantly improve the octane rating of the gas. This allowed them to produce much cheaper grades of fuel and still maintain the needed octane ratings that a car's engine required.

Another benefit that became known over time was that Tetraethyl lead kept valve seats from becoming worn down prematurely. Exhaust valves, in early model cars that were subject to engine knocking, tended to get micro-welds that would get pulled apart on opening. This resulted in rough valve seats and premature failure. Lead helped fuel ignite only when appropriate on the power stroke, thus helping eliminate exhaust valve wear and tear.

The potential health issues with Tetraethyl lead were known even before major oil companies began using it. In 1922, while plans for production of leaded gasoline were just getting underway, Thomas Midgley received a letter from Charles Klaus, a German scientist, stating of lead, "it's a creeping and malicious poison," and warned that it had killed a fellow scientist. This didn't seem to faze Midley, who himself came down with lead poisoning during the planning phase. While recovering in Miami, Midgley wrote to an oil industry engineer that public poisoning was "almost impossible, as no one will repeatedly get their hands covered in gasoline containing lead…" Other opposition to lead came from a lab director for the Public Health Service (a part of the US Department of Health and Human Services) who wrote to the assistant surgeon general stating lead was a "serious menace to public health."

Despite the warnings, production on leaded gasoline began in 1923. It didn't take long for workers to begin succumbing to lead poisoning. At DuPont's manufacturing plant in Deepwater, New Jersey, workers began to fall like dominoes. One worker died in the fall of 1923. Three died in the summer of 1924 and four more in the winter of 1925. Despite this, public controversy didn't begin until five workers died and 44 were hospitalized in October of 1924 at Standard Oils plant in Bayway, New Jersey.

The Public Health Service held a conference in 1925 to address the problem of leaded gasoline. As you would expect, Kettering testified for the use of lead, stating that oil companies could produce alcohol fuels that had the benefits that were provided by lead; however, the volumes needed to supply a growing fuel hungry society could not be met. Alice Hamilton of Harvard University countered proponents of leaded gasoline and testified that this type of fuel was dangerous to people and the environment. In the end, the Public Health Service allowed leaded gasoline to remain on the market.

In 1974, after environmental hazards began to become overwhelmingly apparent, the EPA (Environmental Protection Agency) announced a scheduled phase-out of lead content in gasoline. One way manufacturers met these and other emission standards was to use catalytic converters. Catalytic converters use a chemical reaction to change pollutants, like carbon monoxide and other harmful hydrocarbons, to carbon dioxide, nitrogen and water. Tetraethyl lead would tend to clog these converters, making them inoperable. Thus, unleaded gasoline became the fuel of choice for any car with a catalytic converter.

The requirements by the EPA, emission control mechanisms on cars, and the advent of other octane boosting alternatives spelled the end for widespread leaded gasoline use. Manufacturers soon found that cars could no longer handle such a fuel; public tolerance of the environmental and health hazards would not allow it; and it became cost prohibitive to continue producing it. On January 1, 1996, the Clean Air Act completely banned the use of leaded fuel for any on-road vehicle. Should you be found to possess leaded gasoline in your car, you can be subject to a $10,000 fine.

This hasn't completely gotten rid of leaded gasoline. You are still permitted to use it for off-road vehicles, aircraft, racing cars, farm equipment, and marine engines in the United States.

BONUS FACT

Since the reduction of leaded gas in the United States, the average level of lead in the blood of Americans has decreased by over 75%.

WHY A GECKO'S FEET CAN STICK TO ALMOST ANYTHING

It has been observed since the fourth century BC that geckos have the ability to climb walls, hang upside down, and apparently "stick" to anything. Aristotle was the first person known to have commented on the phenomenon, stating geckos have the ability to "run up and down a tree in any way, even with the head downwards." It wasn't until recently that it was discovered what gave them this Spider-Man-like ability.

Geckos have millions of tiny hairs on their toes called seta ("setae" being Latin for "bristle"). All combined, these hair-like tissues give a washboard type appearance to a gecko's toes. Each one of these seta has thousands of thinner hair-like structures that have flat caps at the ends called spatulae (yes the same meaning as the thing that flips our pancakes). These spatulae use what is called van der Waals' force to allow the gecko's feet to adhere to objects.

More specifically, all of these seta and spatulae combined give the gecko's feet an extremely large surface area, compared to its size. This surface area allows the gecko to take advantage of attraction caused by van der Waals' force. Van der Waals' force, simply stated, is the combined attractive forces between molecules. Normally, the force between molecules is too minute to matter; however, given the light weight nature of a gecko (approximately 2.5 ounces) and the extreme number of spatulae, the combined force allows the gecko to "stick" to almost anything. This surface area is so great that it has been shown that if a mature gecko were to have all of their seta in contact with a surface at one time, it could potentially support up to 290 lbs.

There may be even more going on here as well, though it's still up for debate. A study published in the *Journal of the Royal Society Interface* in the summer of 2011 showed that geckos leave footprints in the form of phospholipid residue. Phospholipids are a type of lipid (molecule that forms fats and waxes) that can form with two layers. These layers allow it to both attract water on one side and repel it on the other. This study suggests that there might be more going on with a gecko's ability than we currently realize, and it is thought by its publishers that these phospholipids might also play a role in a gecko's sticky talent.

While the discovery of phospholipids in the gecko's footprint brings a new factor to the equation, the ancillary evidence that a gecko cannot "stick" to Teflon is a strong indication that van der Waals' force is the main mediator in their abilities. Teflon (Polytetrafluoroethylene) is mainly carbon and fluorine. Fluorine itself is highly electronegative, meaning it really really likes to attract electrons to itself. Because of this, it tends to mitigate what is known as the "London dispersion force." This force is thought to usually be the dominate player in the van der Waals' force. A gecko, which is dependent on the sum total of all of the factors of van der Waals' force, would find it extremely difficult to stick to anything that eliminates its ability to utilize the force. And indeed, geckos cannot "stick" to Teflon.

WHY AMERICA IS CALLED AMERICA

Amerigo Vespucci was a navigator that traveled to "the new world" in 1499 and 1502. Being a well-educated man, he realized that this new world was not part of Asia, as some had initially thought. Vespucci chose to write about his travels, and his books were published in 1502 and 1504. Being both entertaining and educational, his accounts of the new world were reprinted in almost every European language.

In 1507, a German cartographer, Martin Waldseemüller, chose to make a new map that included the new world. He and two scholarly partners were aware of Vespucci's writings but were ignorant of Columbus's expeditions. As such, they mistakenly thought Vespucci discovered this new land and so named it after him, stating:

"But now these parts (Europe, Asia and Africa, the three continents of the Ptolemaic geography) have been extensively explored and a fourth part has been discovered by Americus Vespuccius (the Latin form of Vespucci's name), I do not see what right any one would have to object to calling this part after Americus, who discovered it and who is a man of intelligence, and so to name it Amerige, that is, the Land of Americus, or America: since both Europa and Asia got their names from women."

When the new map, approximately 8 feet by 4 feet, was unveiled by Waldseemüller, it had the large title "AMERICA" across what is now present-day Brazil. Waldseemüller used Vespucci's travelogues as a reference for his drawing, so his map had South America as the only part of this new western hemisphere. When North America was later added, the mapmakers of the time retained the original name. In 1538, the famous geographer Gerard Mercator chose to name the entire north and south parts of America as one large "America" for the entire western hemisphere.

Christopher Columbus might well have had the new world named after him had it not been for two shortcomings. The first was that Columbus was under the mistaken impression that he had found a new route to Asia and was not aware that America was an entirely new continent. The second was that at this time the masses were not widely aware of his travels. Had they been, Mr.

Waldseemüller and his colleagues might have named it Columba! Of course, had the Norsemen's previous journeys to the "New World" (and possibly Muslim and Chinese explorers before) been widely known, another name might have been chosen altogether. As it happened, Vespucci did write about it and was the first to call this land the "Novus Mundus" (Latin for "New World").

WHY GARLIC MAKES BREATH SMELL BAD

There are a few things going on to cause this bad smell, but principally the root cause is various sulfuric compounds from the garlic. Initially, most of the bad breath resulting from eating garlic comes directly from the sulfuric compounds introduced into your mouth. Garlic also promotes the growth of some of the microbes in your mouth that already cause bad breath, which further exacerbates the problem.

You may have noticed that even if you brush your teeth, rinse with mouthwash, and other such methods to clean out these compounds and various microbes from your mouth, the bad breath caused by garlic still remains to some extent. This has to do with the fact that some of these sulfuric compounds get metabolized, eventually making their way into your blood stream.

The primary smelly culprit here has been found to be allyl methyl sulfide, which is passed into the blood during the digestive process. Once it's in your blood, it eventually gets passed out of your body through various bodily excretions, which includes being exuded through your pores and also passed into the air that fills your lungs. So as you breathe, the air goes into your lungs and is contaminated by the allyl methyl sulfide; this in turn causes your breath to continue to smell even if you've cleaned your mouth out.

As mentioned, this sulfuric compound will not only find its way into the air in your lungs, but also will be exuded from your pores. This causes your whole body to smell, not just your breath. As you are excreting this sulfide, you essentially are wearing a stinky perfume. This effect lasts as long as it takes for your body to get rid of the stinky sulfuric compounds, which can be anywhere from a few hours to as much as a day after eating the garlic.

BONUS FACT

Because of the fact that the smelly sulfuric compounds from the garlic are in your blood, there is little you can do to immediately get rid of the smell from eating garlic, other than to mask it with a stronger smell. However, many people swear by parsley and sprigs for getting rid of garlic breath, which is why parsley is often included in many dishes that contain significant amounts of garlic. Another popular cover up is to drink hot mint tea. Further, drinking milk while eating something garlicky has been shown to reduce bad breath and does an even better job if you drink the milk while the garlicky item is still in your mouth and swish it around.

WHY POOP IS BROWN

Poop is brown due to bile from your gall bladder being metabolized by the bacteria in your intestines. This results in a by-product called stercobilin, which, in turn, makes poop look brown-ish.

Without this stercobilin, your poop would typically look grey-ish/white. Because of this, a sure sign you are having problems with bile production, such as a blocked bile duct by a gall stone or something more serious like pancreatic cancer, is if you notice your poop is this white/grey-ish color.

In the end, brown poop is a pretty good sign you are a relatively healthy individual. Some other common poop colors that generally aren't a good sign of health are as follows:

- If you notice your poop is red, this could be a sign of internal bleeding or could just mean you've recently eaten beets. If the cause is bleeding and the bleeding is from your stomach or throat, however, your poop won't be red, but rather black and will smell worse than that time you decided you should eat a box of Twinkies and a box of Cheesy Handi-Snacks all in one sitting.

- Yellow poop means there is a lot of fat in your feces. This is not a good sign. Consider turning this into a positive by making poop candles with your fatty deposits. Yellow poop also has a very strong odor, which will give your poo-candles that little something extra.

- Green poop is an indicator of some sort of bacterial infection or that you have recently eaten a lot of leafy foods.

WHY THERE IS BRAILLE ON DRIVE UP ATMS

Mainly, it is because it is required by law, thanks to the ADA Accessibility Guidelines for Buildings and Facilities. There are certain exceptions to these requirements when it comes to drive-up ATMs vs. walk-up ATMs, such as the differing requirements on the "Reach Ranges" in section 4.34.3. However, getting rid of the Braille is not one of these exceptions, despite initial protests from the American Banker's Association who argued that any visually impaired person could simply get the driver to help. The committee in charge of developing these standards rejected this argument because it would no longer allow a visually impaired person to use the ATM independently.

You'll also often hear people say that the reason behind including Braille on drive-up ATMs has to do with being "cheaper to make one ATM machine, rather than two different models" or in a similar vein "cheaper to have one set of buttons with Braille, than one with and one without." This may or may not be true, but given that the American Bankers Association fought to try to remove requirements to make the drive-up ATMs accessible to the visually impaired, it would seem this "cheaper" factor, if it exists, wasn't a contributing factor in the switch, presumably because when factoring in the cost of replacing the older non-Braille ATMs, the cost of "one design / set of buttons" wasn't enough of a benefit for the ABA.

In the end, blind people actually do use drive-up ATMs all the time, contrary to what many people think. It's not uncommon at all for them to run errands in a taxi-cab, for instance. When they do, a drive-up ATM is certainly more convenient for a blind person, given someone can drive them right up to the ATM. And they probably wouldn't want to trust the cab driver with their card and pin number.

Up until somewhat recently, a related question would have been, "why do walk-up ATMs have Braille when many ATMs don't have any facility for letting the blind person know what is happening on the screen?" This situation has since been improved, but for a long time, there was no set way to make the interaction with the ATM, beyond the Braille, accessible to the visually impaired. Initially, no one was really sure what the best way to handle this aspect of accessibility would be, so the Accessibility Guidelines didn't address it.

Thus, in the early days, quite a lot of banks simply provided a Braille instruction manual for a given ATM and the visually impaired user would need to follow the steps exactly to do a certain task and hope nothing went wrong or that the ATM didn't suddenly get a software update that changed that interaction. These instructions can still be found on many ATMs, but today there is also, generally, some sort of audible system to let the visually impaired user know what's happening on the screen (usually through a headphone jack, for privacy).

WHY SWISS CHEESE HAS HOLES

The holes come from a by-product of some of the microbes added to milk to make Swiss cheese. Specifically, there are three primary types of bacteria that are typically used to make Swiss cheese (these can vary slightly depending on the manufacturer): Streptococcus thermophilus; Lactobacillus helveticus; and Propionibacterium shermanii.

The first two types of microbes produce significant amounts of lactic acid, which is, in turn, consumed by the latter type of microbes, Propionibacterium shermanii. It is this Propionibacterium shermanii that is responsible for the holes in Swiss cheese. Through the process of consuming the lactic acid, the shermanii produces acetate, propionic acid, and carbon dioxide as a by-product.

The acetate and propionic acid give the Swiss cheese much of its distinct flavor, while the carbon dioxide forms bubbles within the cheese block or wheel. These carbon dioxide bubbles are left in as the cheese continues to ferment, rather than pressing them out, which gives Swiss cheese its distinctive holes. Historically, however, these holes were seen as an imperfection in the cheese and most manufacturers would try to avoid them by pressing this type of cheese during the aging process to force the bubbles out and keep the cheese solid throughout the block or wheel.

BONUS FACT

The size of the holes in Swiss cheese sold in the United States is regulated by the U.S. government. This is widely criticized by many Swiss cheese manufactures outside of the U.S., particularly in Switzerland, which tend to produce their cheese in a non-factory environment and thus, take more pride in the end product, rather than the bottom line. The reason for the protest is that the size of the holes is regulated by varying the curing time, acidity, and temperature, during the fermentation process, which typically lasts 60-100 days. These changes, however, also will significantly affect the texture and flavor of the cheese itself. Many foreign Swiss cheese manufactures claim that the regulations put forth by the American government produce an inferior flavored Swiss cheese, hence the protest.

The U.S. government created these regulations at the behest of commercial American Swiss cheese producers, who were having problems with their mechanical slicers cutting cheese when the Swiss cheese holes were too big, (typical sizes of the holes used to be around the size of a nickel). Rather than innovate or upgrade their equipment, they went with the age-old practice of simply lobbying the government to make laws to fix their problem. Namely, to specify that, in order for Swiss cheese to be classified as "Grade A," which is generally necessary for high-volume sales in the United States, it must have holes no bigger than 3/8 of an inch, which was about half the typical size before these new regulations were put in place. This also significantly shortens the required aging time of North American style Swiss cheese, which also benefited the American mass-producers of the cheese.

WHY CATS LIKE CATNIP

Catnip, which is a perennial herb in the mint family, contains a chemical called "nepetalactone" that is released when catnip is crushed. When cats get a whiff of nepetalactone, most will start rubbing themselves against it, playing with it, sometimes eating it, and generally will act quite bizarrely. It is thought, but not known exactly, that this chemical mimics certain feline pheromones, specifically their theoretical facial pheromones. (It isn't known whether these actually exist, but many researchers think they do.)

Once cats have been exposed to the nepetalactone for a few minutes, the chemical loses its effect on them, and cats will usually no longer be interested in it for about an hour or two. At this point the chemical will start to kick in again as the cats breathe it in, and they will once again begin acting bizarrely around it for a few minutes.

Despite the apparent drug-like effect, it isn't thought that catnip is in any way harmful to cats, nor is it thought that it is addictive. Most researches think that nepetalactone simply triggers something in their brains that causes them to want to rub up against this particular smell, not unlike what dogs often do when they encounter certain smells. That being said, cats can "overdose" on catnip, which typically results in vomiting or diarrhea.

Interestingly, not all cats respond to catnip. Whatever genetic quirk that causes them to respond to nepetalactone is inherited and only about 70% of cats show a behavioral difference around catnip. Further, cats under the age of a few weeks old are also not attracted to catnip, and some even show an aversion to it.

Not only are very young cats sometimes averse to catnip, but so are cockroaches, mosquitoes, flies, and termites. In fact, nepetalactone extract has been shown to be ten times more effective at repelling mosquitoes than DEET (N-Diethyl-meta-toluamide), which is the chemical traditionally used in mosquito repellant. However, it should be noted that when put on human skin, nepetalactone's effectiveness as a mosquito repellant decreases drastically, so it's more suitable as a mosquito repellent when sprayed on clothing or the like.

WHY COKE TRIED TO SWITCH TO "NEW COKE"

It turns out there was actually (if you squint at the problem hard enough), a semi-good reason for making the switch. It didn't work out, of course… But then, it kind of did work out amazingly well at the same time, as you'll soon see.

Now, before I get into the real reason for the switch, let me debunk the conspiracy theory that Coca Cola was trying to swindle people into accepting high fructose corn syrup over sugar in their drink by pulling the New Coke stunt. The truth of the matter is that they'd already allowed bottlers to use high fructose corn syrup in Coke for about five years before they introduced New Coke (before they even thought up the idea to make a New Coke).

Most bottlers made the switch pretty quickly because of the drastic cost savings. Initially, Coca-Cola allowed a 50% corn syrup substitution and by about 6 months before the introduction of New Coke, nearly every major bottler of Coca-Cola was using 100% high fructose corn syrup, rather than sugar or a mixture of the two. So those who claimed they could taste a difference because of the high fructose corn syrup after the return of the old Coca-Cola, actually had already been drinking it with high fructose corn syrup, in most cases long before New Coke.

Coca-Cola did consider not announcing that they were switching to New Coke, with a plan to just very gradually change the flavor. But they ended up deciding that it was too risky, because if someone noticed, it might become a huge news story and hurt sales from the bad publicity of trying to trick their customers.

So what really was the motivation for switching to New Coke? Coke had steadily been losing ground to Pepsi and by the early 1980s, taste tests done by Coca-Cola and Pepsi showed that most people tested preferred Pepsi over Coke. Further, if not for Coke's exclusive contracts with many restaurants and vending machine vendors, Pepsi would have been drastically outselling Coke, as it was in supermarkets and other locations where people had a choice.

Coca-Cola, thus, set about changing their formula to come up with something people would prefer over the original Coke and

Pepsi. Specifically, they created New Coke based on their Diet Coke formula. Diet Coke was extremely popular right from its debut (rocketing up to the third most popular cola after Pepsi and Coke within just a few years of its launch), even though it was a new flavor and not based on regular Coke, as the name seems to imply.

Thus, as taste tests showed that more people preferred the taste of Diet Coke to regular Coke, they decided to primarily just take out the artificial sweeteners in Diet Coke and substituted in high fructose corn syrup. With a few more minor modifications, they succeeded in creating a new apparently tasty drink.

This wasn't a case of them not doing their due diligence on whether it was better than the original Coca-Cola. They knew full well how big of a thing it would be to abandon their old formulation. As such, they ran numerous tests that showed the vast majority of people preferred the new formulation over the old and it also beat out Pepsi by a decent margin.

What went wrong is still partially up for debate, but the heart of the issue is basically the "nostalgia" factor and that they'd spent nearly a century marketing their product as something you can't live without, then they took it away. People had apparently taken this message to heart. While the taste tests made New Coke look great, they never explicitly asked the question in any of their tests "Would you care if we switched in this new formulation of Coke and got rid of the old?" They didn't do this because they didn't want people to know they were developing a new formula at all.

They did ask a very similar question that subtly implied the previous question and the result should have clued them in to the dissent. They asked tasters who had liked it, "Would you buy this [new flavor] if it were Coca-Cola?" While the majority said yes, about 10% said no and got angry about the subtle implication of getting rid of Coke. While this is a small percentage, the problem ahead was illustrated in that these 10% were very vocal about their dissent and had a tendency to try to convince other testers that they should switch their answer to "no" too.

This is exactly how it played out when New Coke was introduced. At first, sales were up a significant amount over the previous year, even more than Coca-Cola expected; and according to surveys run by Coca-Cola, most people preferred the new flavor over the old. Just as importantly, the majority of existing Coke drinkers continued to buy Coke at the same levels as they did before. Further, most of those few customers they lost weren't switching to Pepsi, they were simply just not drinking Coke anymore. Coca-Cola stock went up and things were looking really good.

But then the vocal minority started kicking up their heels; complaints trickled in and the angered Coke fans started enlisting the aid of the media. Soon that trickle developed into a flood. One man, Gay Mullins, even started the Old Cola Drinkers of America organization to lobby for the return of the Old Coke, or at the least try to get Coca-Cola to license out the formula to someone else. The fact that in a blind taste test Mullins himself picked New Coke over Old Coke as his favorite didn't stop him from attempting to sue Coca-Cola over the switch.

The dissenters started convincing others; many who had never even tried New Coke decided they hated it before even tasting it, primarily because they were upset at the fact that the original Coke was no longer available. Finally, just three months after New Coke was introduced, the public outcry forced Coca-Cola to release the old formula under the name "Coca-Cola Classic".

So why did they get rid of Coca-Cola "Classic" in the first place, rather than just introducing New Coke as a separate drink right off the bat? There were a few reasons, but the big one was because the market for cola drinks at the time was shrinking fast and by introducing another Coke substitute (having introduced Diet Coke in 1982), they feared it would split the market for their product with many people who would have drank Coca-Cola Classic now drinking New Coke. This would allow Pepsi to take the top spot by a good margin, allowing Pepsi to not only claim taste tests showed people preferred Pepsi, but also to boast about how Pepsi was the most popular soft drink in the world. Coca-Cola was unwilling to give this marketing advantage to Pepsi, so decided to get rid of the original Coke, in favor of New Coke. After all, every test they ran showed people preferred the new formulation anyways. What could go wrong?

Despite this switch not working out the way they hoped, it did in the end work out amazingly well. After this fiasco, Coca-Cola Classic, instead of continuing its steady decline, began to take back market share over both Pepsi and New Coke. This was despite the fact that when people were blind taste tested, they continued to almost universally pick both New Coke and Pepsi as better tasting than Coca-Cola Classic. Some theorize that the taste tests here are flawed because they often only gave people small sips. Thus, the sweeter tasting Pepsi and New Coke would perform better, whereas when drunk normally, might be too sweet, and so Coca-Cola would win in these cases. Those who theorize this is the reason for Coke losing out in the taste tests tend to state that Pepsi's steady rise before this fiasco was not due to superior taste, but from their superior marketing, particularly to youth.

Whatever the case, while the whole thing was a fiasco that looked for a time like it might kill the brand, six months after the return of the original Coke, Coca-Cola sales had risen to double the rate of Pepsi and it continued to climb. Thus, the blunder ultimately was a huge part of why Coca-Cola was able to reestablish itself as the most popular cola in the world. Sometimes doing something stupid can really pay off.

BONUS FACT

Despite New Coke sales dropping like crazy after the return of Classic Coke, when the Wall Street Journal in 1987 did yet another blind taste test of Pepsi, Classic Coke, and New Coke, with most of the participants before the test saying they preferred one or the other of Coke or Pepsi, New Coke won out as the most popular choice again. Much like the New Coke dissenters, when the people were told they'd picked New Coke as their favorite instead of their previous stated favorites of Coke or Pepsi, rather than deciding they'd start drinking New Coke, they predominately got angry at the testers.

WHY POP ROCKS POP

Much like other hard sugar candies, Pop Rocks are made primarily of sugar, corn syrup, water, and artificial flavoring. What causes the candy to pop when it comes in contact with the moisture and heat in your mouth is not due to any ingredient. Rather, it is due to the way the candy is made.

Basically, what they do is heat the ingredients together, bringing the mixture to boil. They continue to boil it until the moisture level descends suitably so that a thick syrupy substance remains. In normal hard sugar candies, this substance is then put in molds and allowed to cool and harden. With pop rocks, they expose the hot mix to carbon dioxide at about 600 pounds per square inch worth of pressure. This causes very small bubbles of carbon dioxide to form within the mix. The substance is then cooled and subsequently hardens.

Once the hard candy is formed, the pressure is released. This causes the candy to shatter, leaving small nuggets of hard candy, which are the Pop Rocks. Many of these nuggets still contain pockets of carbon dioxide kept at relatively high pressure. When the candy hits the saliva in your mouth, it quickly dissolves the thin barriers containing the pressurized carbon dioxide. This results in the bubbles bursting fairly quickly, releasing the trapped carbon dioxide, often with sufficient force to cause the candy to pop and sometimes jump in your mouth.

BONUS FACT

Pop Rocks were invented by Chemist William A. Mitchell, who worked for General Foods. He also invented Tang, Cool Whip, quick-setting Jell-O, a tapioca substitute, and powdered egg whites, among other things. In total, he received over 70 patents in his lifetime.

WHY WE CALL A CRAZY PERSON A "BASKET CASE"

At first, "basket case" didn't mean someone who was crazy. Instead, it referred to someone who had a physical disability. The phrase has its origins in World War I. Funny enough, one of the earliest known documented instances of the phrase was actually in denial that "basket cases" actually existed, as found in a bulletin issued in March of 1919 on behalf of the United States Surgeon General:

"The Surgeon General of the Army... denies...that there is any foundation for the stories that have been circulated...of the existence of basket cases in our hospitals."

But just what was the Surgeon General referring to when he said "basket case"? When this bulletin came out, many newspapers felt the need to define the phrase for their audiences, so apparently the phrase wasn't widely used at this point. They defined it as "a soldier who has lost both arms and legs and therefore must be carried in a basket." (The Syracuse Herald, March of 1919)

Whether they were literally carried around in baskets as the newspapers stated or the phrase originally was just referencing the then common colloquial idea of associating baskets with beggars or helplessness, given the grisly nature of the First World War and anecdotal reports, it seems plausible enough that there probably were at least some "basket cases," despite the Surgeon General's denial.

As you can imagine, the original meaning of "basket case" was never incredibly common. It wasn't until World War II that the phrase prominently resurfaced. Near the end of the war in May of 1944, once again, the Surgeon General attempted to deny that there were any basket cases:

"...there is nothing to rumors of so-called 'basket cases'—cases of men with both arms and legs amputated."

After World War II, the original meaning fell out of favor altogether, likely due to the lack of literal basket cases. However, for a while the phrase expanded to mean someone with a physical disability who was unable to get around by themselves easily.

Today, of course, it has further evolved to mostly be a slang phrase for someone with a mental disability, or someone who seems to have been moved to act in a crazy fashion for whatever reason.

BONUS FACT

Another slightly less well-known usage of the phrase today is to describe a business or organization that has been rendered helpless in some way—such as filing for bankruptcy.

WHY THERE IS AN AREA OF NEW YORK CALLED "THE BRONX"

This is thanks to a seventeenth century Scandinavian man by the name of Jonas Bronck, originally from Tórshavn in the Faroe Islands.

In 1639, Bronck immigrated to New Amsterdam in New Netherland, which was right next to what is today called Bronx River, named after Jonas Bronck.

Why? In New Amsterdam, Bronck owned a 680 acre farm which was called, unimaginatively, "Bronck's Land" and the river abutting it "Bronck's River." He held this land for just four years before dying in 1643. From there, various people owned this property, keeping the name Bronck's Land, until Colonel Lewis Morris acquired it and renamed it the "Manor of Morrisania."

Despite the renaming of the land, the river next to it continued to be called "Bronck's River." From the river's name, the modern-day name of "Bronx" got extended to the region directly around the river in the late nineteenth century. The name for the region has stuck ever since.

BONUS FACT

As to why it's "Bronx" instead of "Bronck's," this isn't clear, but the switch happened around the same time there was a big push for the simplification of English; remnants of this can be seen today in the names of the Boston Red Sox and the Chicago White Sox (instead of "Socks"). It may be that the switch from "Bronck's" to "Bronx" happened for the same reason, though this is just speculation, and I could find no direct documented evidence of this; so take it with a grain of salt. But the time period (the late nineteenth to early twentieth century) of the switch, at least, matches up.

WHY NEW YORK CITY IS CALLED "THE BIG APPLE"

The earliest documented reference to New York being referred to as "The Big Apple" comes from a 1909 book by Edward Martin, called *The Wayfarer*. In it, he uses the moniker in a metaphorical sense, rather than a proper name for the city:

"Kansas is apt to see in New York a greedy city… It inclines to think that the big apple gets a disproportionate share of the national sap…"

The next known documented instance of New York being called "The Big Apple" comes from sportswriter John J. Fitz Gerald who began popularizing the name starting on May 3, 1921, where he stated in a column:

"J. P. Smith, with Tippity Witchet and others of the L. T. Bauer string, is scheduled to start for 'the big apple' to-morrow after a most prosperous Spring campaign at Bowie and Havre de Grace."

In this case, he was referencing the early 1920s practice of calling certain race courses in the New York City region this particular fruity name, in that the New York City races tended to payout significant prizes to the winner compared to races in many other regions, hence "big apple."

According to linguist Dr. Gerald Cohen, this wasn't out of the ordinary, even outside of horse racing. As he states, "Apples were important throughout history, but the big red delicious apples developed in Iowa in the 1870s came to be regarded as extra special. That led to 'the big apple' being applied to things and people who were extra special, or perhaps only thought they were…"

As to applying this to New York City, it's thought that Fitz Gerald didn't come up with this on his own but rather heard it from people from New Orleans in 1920 when he traveled down to that city to supposedly sell one of his horses, with the common tale being that it came from a couple of stable hands.

Fitz Gerald explicitly mentions this three years later in his 1923 column "Around the Big Apple," though it's possible he just made the story up:

"The Big Apple. The dream of every lad that ever threw a leg over a thoroughbred and the goal of all horsemen. There's only one Big Apple. That's New York. Two dusky stable hands were leading a pair of thoroughbred around the 'cooling rings' of adjoining stables at the Fair Grounds in New Orleans and engaging in desultory conversation. 'Where y'all goin' from here?' queried one. 'From here we're headin' for The Big Apple,' proudly replied the other. 'Well, you'd better fatten up them skinners or all you'll get from the apple will be the core,' was the quick rejoinder."

This nickname for New York City gradually caught on and began being used in a non-sporting sense, including a popular song/dance coming out in the 1930s called "The Big Apple," as well as numerous references in other songs, particularly in jazz music.

However, this nickname for the city died off by the 1960s and few outside of the city would have understood the reference had you used it then. That all changed in the 1970s when Charles Gillett and the New York Convention and Visitors Bureau decided to revive the nickname in a tourism campaign. In this campaign, they began aggressively advertising New York City as a tourist hotspot and referred to it as "The Big Apple," using bright, clean looking red apples in their advertisements to attempt to contrast the popular notion of the day that New York City was a dirty place where you were as likely to be mugged as not if you visited there.

BONUS FACT

If you've been in New York City since 1997, you might notice the corner of 54th and Broadway is called "Big Apple Corner." This is in homage to Fitz Gerald who lived near there for nearly three decades, from 1934 to 1963 when he died.

WHY MOSQUITO BITES ITCH

When female mosquitoes poke their proboscis through your skin so they can suck some of your blood, they inject you with some of their saliva. This saliva helps them to drink your blood more quickly, as it contains a cocktail of anticoagulants. Once the female mosquito is full up of your blood or is disturbed, she flies away, leaving some of her saliva behind. Your body then kicks your immune system into high gear as a response to the presence of this saliva, producing various antibodies that, in turn, bind to the antigens in the mosquito's saliva.

This also triggers the release of histamine. Histamine is a nitrogen compound that, among other things, triggers an inflammatory response. It also helps white blood cells and other proteins to engage invaders in your body by making the capillaries of these cells more permeable. Bottom line, the histamine ends up making the blood vessels near the bite swell up, producing a pink, itchy bump where the mosquito poked you.

Scratching the bump only makes this worse because it causes more irritation and inflammation of the sight, resulting in your immune system thinking it needs more antibodies to get rid of the foreign protein. So the more you scratch, the more it will swell; the itchier it will get; and the longer it will last.

BONUS FACT

Only female mosquitoes drink blood. They don't need the blood for their own nourishment; rather, they need it to be able to produce eggs. Once the female has safely acquired a "blood meal", she will rest for a few days while her body develops the eggs from digesting the proteins and iron in the blood, producing amino acids which are used as the building blocks for the synthesis of the egg yolk proteins. So what do mosquitoes eat? Male and female mosquitoes alike get their nourishment from plant nectar and other sugar sources

.

WHY YOU GENERALLY SHOULDN'T PUT METALS IN A MICROWAVE

First, it should be noted that it is not unsafe to put all metals in the microwave. Indeed, you often put metals in the microwave, such as when you put a hot pocket in the little pouch and place it in the microwave. The pouch has a thin layer of aluminum lining the inside that is designed to absorb the microwave radiation and heat up to brown the outside of the hot pocket.

On top of that, the inside walls of your microwave oven are made of metal. This forms something called a Faraday Cage that traps the microwaves inside the box so that they cook the food and not things around the microwave oven, like you. If you look closely, you'll also see that the window you look at the food through has metal mesh lining it. The holes in this mesh are smaller than the wavelengths of the electromagnetic radiation your microwave is producing. This makes it so the waves can't pass through the holes. Visible light, however, is comprised of much smaller wavelengths, so that form of radiated energy passes through the holes just fine, allowing you to see inside your microwave while it's running without getting your eyeballs cooked.

So if the inside of your microwave is lined with metal and certain food products have containers that contain metal, such as hot pockets and pot pies, why does your microwave manual say not to put metal in the microwave?

First, you'll need to understand a little about how a microwave oven actually works. At its core, a microwave oven is a pretty simple device. It's basically just a magnetron hooked up to a high voltage source. This magnetron creates microwaves which are directed into the metal box. These generated microwaves then bounce around inside the microwave until they are absorbed via dielectric loss in various molecules resulting in the molecules heating up. Types of matter that work well here are things such as water, ceramics, certain polymers, etc. These all convert microwave energy into heat quite effectively.

Metals, on the other hand, are great conductors of electricity, being packed with electrons that can move freely. Depending on the shape/type/thickness/distribution/etc. of metal, you may observe some heating of the metal itself in the microwave or none at all. You may also observe some arcing of electricity or none at all. When these microwaves hit the metal, free electrons on the surface of the metal end up moving from side to side very rapidly. This, in turn, prevents the electric wave from entering the metal; thus, the waves end up being reflected instead. However, there is also the potential that this will create a sufficient charge density that the electrical potential in the metal object exceeds the dielectric breakdown of air. When this happens, it will result in arcing inside your microwave, from that metal to another electrical conductor with lower potential (often the wall of the microwave). In extreme cases, these electrical sparks can damage the wall by burning small holes in it. It can also end up burning out the magnetron in your microwave oven or, in modern microwaves, can provide a surge that damages sensitive microelectronics, possibly killing your microwave or making it unsafe to use.

Another way it can kill the magnetron of your microwave is when enough of the generated microwaves don't get absorbed, such as if the food is wrapped in aluminum foil or mostly enclosed in a metal container. This can create a lot of energy that does not get absorbed and has nowhere to go but back to the magnetron, damaging it.

On a more mundane level, something like a spoon or a metal plate or the like, positioned correctly, will simply make your food potentially not cook normally. On that note, it is once again, actually acceptable to put metal in a microwave under the proper conditions. Some microwaves even have metal grates inside for setting food on, such as is often the case with certain convection ovens. There are also certain types of metal pots and pans that are microwave safe. These all, however, are carefully designed to not cause any problems in your microwave oven. In general, putting metal in the microwave is unsafe, not because you are necessarily at risk of bodily harm (though in extreme cases a fire might be started from this), but primarily because it has the potential of damaging your microwave.

WHY SOAP OPERAS ARE CALLED "SOAP OPERAS"

This all started in the 1920s; a simpler time where Jazz was swell; the Soviet Union was in its infancy; Robbert Goddard became the first rocket man; and the world only existed in black and white... apparently.

In this bustling time, radio was the Bee's Knees. On the radio was a series of serials aimed at women, aired during the day time. Dame's thought these were the cat's meow and ate up every second of them.

To fund the shows, the radio networks began seeking out certain companies to sponsor the episodes. Now these dolls were no dumb Dora's, so the networks particularly sought to match the advertisements closely with their target audience to get a good response, and make a few more clams from the deal. This campaign hit on all sixes and made these shows extremely profitable.

Among the first major sponsors of these serials were soap manufacturers Procter & Gamble, Colgate-Palmolive, and Lever Brothers. Because so many of the sponsors were soap manufacturers, the media started calling these shows "soap operas."

WHY POPCORN POPS

First a little background. Popcorn or "zea mays everta" is a special kind of Flint corn, also known as "Indian corn" and sometimes "Calico corn." Flint corn is readily recognizable as the kernels have a hard outer shell, likened to flint, hence the name. This hard outer shell is essential in making popcorn kernels pop. In fact, popcorn is the only type of corn that will pop.

So why does popcorn pop? There are three main elements of popcorn that have to come together to produce popcorn kernels that are good for popping. Those three elements are: the percentage of water content; a hard, undamaged, water impermeable shell; and a starchy center.

When the kernels are heated up, the water inside begins to steam. Assuming the water impermeable shell doesn't have any cracks in it to let the steam escape, this creates a simple little steam/pressure cooker. If the kernels aren't heated too quickly to their bursting point, the starch inside the kernel will turn into a kind of gel-like substance. At around 350-450 degrees Fahrenheit, the pressure of the steam gets so great that the hard shell bursts, with the needed pressure typically around 135 psi. When this happens, the steam rapidly expands, which results in the gel expanding out and hardening into airy foam.

Specifically, as the gelatinized starch expands, it forms thin airy bubbled jelly. These jelly bubbles will fuse together and then solidify very quickly as they are exposed to air and cool off. The cooling sets the starch and protein polymers into the white puffy flakes we all know and love.

WHY THE HOTTEST PART OF THE SUMMER IS CALLED THE "DOG DAYS"

The earliest reference to some aspect of this expression goes all the way back to the ancient Egyptians. They noted that the heliacal rising of the star Sirius heralded the hottest part of the summer. However, it isn't exactly known why the ancient Egyptians associated this star with a dog (the star's hieroglyph is a dog). Sirius would appear in Egypt, after about a 70 day absence, just before the season where the Nile typically floods. So it is thought the star's hieroglyphic symbol being a dog symbolized a "watchdog".

On the other hand, it's very possible that it was for the same reason the ancient Greeks and ancient Romans would also eventually associate this star with a dog. Namely, that it is the brightest star in what is now known as the Canis Major (Latin for "Greater Dog" or "Big Dog") constellation. This constellation simply looks a little bit like a dog, and Sirius is the brightest star in the constellation. So the star got named the "Dog Star," and its heliacal rising marked the start of the hottest part of the year, which then became the "Dog Days."

The Roman's expression for Dog Days was diēs caniculārēs (Latin for "Dog Days"). The Greeks also had a similar expression that literally translated to "Dog Days." They both believed that when Sirius rose around the same time as the Sun, it contributed to that time of year becoming hotter. As such, they would often make sacrifices to Sirius, including sacrificing dogs, to appease Sirius with the hope that this would result in a mild summer and would protect their crops from scorching.

BONUS FACT

Sirius-A is the brightest star visible to the naked eye from Earth, being almost twice as bright as Canopus. Sirius-A and Sirius-B combine to form a binary system and appear as one star to the naked eye, though the vast majority of luminosity to the naked eye comes from Sirius-A, Sirius-B being a white dwarf that is only around 30 AU (astronomical units) away from Sirius-A. It is also theorized that there is a Sirius-C; but to date, this has not been proven. Sirius A and B (and possibly C) combine to form a bright point known as Sirius. If you're wondering, yes, Sirius Black, in Harry Potter, is thought to have been named after the white dwarf, Sirius B. The relationship is further extended by the fact the character Sirius Black was an animagus that could change into a dog.

WHY MEN'S BIKES HAVE A HORIZONTAL CROSSBAR AND WOMEN'S USUALLY DON'T

It would seem that having a slanted crossbar like on women's bikes would make much more sense for men's bikes, decreasing the chance of racking the guy if he does something like slip off the pedals. However, there is actually a really good reason to have a horizontal crossbar on a bike; namely, the horizontal crossbar ends up adding quite a bit of strength to the frame of the bike. This was particularly important in some of the early bikes, which were often made of significantly weaker materials than modern day frames, occasionally even being made of wood.

The problem with this horizontal crossbar was that women all used to wear dresses. So when a woman wanted to get on a bike, she'd have to lift her leg over the bike frame's crossbar, which was quite scandalous for the time as it often exposed a bit of leg and possibly some underwear under her dress. Thus, bike makers began making bike models just for women that slanted the top crossbar down so that the women could mount and dismount the bikes without lifting their legs very high. Modifying the crossbar like that significantly weakened the frames of the bicycles, but this was considered acceptable as it wasn't very lady like for women to ride their bikes as roughly as some men anyways.

This tradition has continued to this day, even though most women don't go around riding bikes in dresses or skirts anymore. For the most part on modern bikes this weakening of the frame by slanting the crossbar isn't significant enough to cause any concern for the bike's structural integrity, even on rough terrain, given modern materials that the frames are made of. Indeed, many BMX bikes for men are now designed with the slanted crossbar to reduce the chance of injury while doing tricks.

Among high-end bikes made for women, this tradition of not having a horizontal crossbar is starting to go away, even though the added strength from a horizontal crossbar isn't typically necessary anymore, particularly with carbon fiber frames. Although, in extremely high end bikes where every gram counts, this can be a factor in illuminating some material. On these high-end bikes, the differences between the men's and the women's bikes now tend to be reflected in the design by accounting for the shorter torsos and arms on most women, modified hip placement, modified seat design, and things of this nature.

WHY POTATOES ARE ALSO CALLED "SPUDS"

Among other definitions, a "spud" is a "sharp, narrow spade" used to dig up large rooted plants. Around the mid-nineteenth century (first documented reference in 1845 in New Zealand), this implement of destruction began lending its name to one of the things it was often used to dig up, namely potatoes. This caught on throughout the English-speaking world and this slang term for a potato is still common to this day.

A false origin you might hear of how potatoes first began being called "spuds" is that it came from the nineteenth century group "The Society for the Prevention of an Unwholesome Diet" (SPUD), who, among other things, felt potatoes shouldn't be eaten. Besides that the real origin is known and well documented, previous to the mid-twentieth century, while abbreviations were prevalent in text, pronouncing them as words was not something people typically did, being something of a very modern phenomenon. In fact, according to linguist David Wilton, "There is only one known pre-twentieth-century [English] word with an acronymic origin and it was in vogue for only a short time in 1886. The word is "colinderies" or "colinda," an acronym for the Colonial and Indian Exposition held in London in that year."

No surprise then that the word "acronym" didn't pop up until 1943.

Beyond referring to potatoes, the ultimate origin of the word "spud" isn't known, first showing up in English around 1440 referring to a short dagger, possibly from the Dutch "spyd", the Old Norse "spjot" (spear), or the Latin "spad-" (sword). Whatever the case, after the fifteenth century, the word expanded from meaning "a short dagger" to also referring to various types of digging implements and eventually to those tubers we all know and love: potatoes.

WHY BEANS GIVE YOU GAS

It's the job of your digestive system to break down the foods you take in, allowing the nutrients to "cross-over" into the different body systems and organs for use as fuel. Each different part breaks these foods down differently. For example, the mouth chews it up into smaller parts, and the stomach uses enzymes and acids to further break it down. The food then goes to the small intestine where most of the nutrients that come from our food (proteins, fats, and carbohydrates) get absorbed into the bloodstream by a process called diffusion. What is left over is then passed to the large intestine whose main job is the absorption of water that remains in the indigestible residue of food. A smaller role of the large intestine is also to break down polysaccharides (fiber) that gets passed into it. One type of fiber prevalent in beans is oligosaccharides.

Oligosaccharides are basically sugar molecules that are made up of several different types of monosaccharides (usually 2-10) to form a polymer. An enzyme that would break these molecules down does not exist anywhere inside the human body. Therefore, when they pass into the large intestine, they serve as food for the countless microbes present. While the microbes are processing these substances, they release several different types of gases, mainly hydrogen, nitrogen and carbon dioxide. Don't be concerned about these particular gases, they are stench-free! Your fetid flatulence affliction is from a different source. Specifically, about one-third of the microbes end up producing methane as a result of breaking down these sugars. Once the methane builds up to the point that it begins to produce pressure on your anal sphincter... That's when the smelly magic happens...

Microbes breaking down these otherwise indigestible substances is important for our health as one of the by-products of this is the creation of various vitamins that get absorbed into the body, as well as for the production of antibodies that help fight off certain types of infections. The downside is that the gaseous side effect of these bacterial processes tends to clear rooms everywhere.

You might have resigned yourself to the fact you can never eat beans before going on a first date, but fret not! There are some methods to prevent your noxious abdominal expulsions. For instance, there is a type of mold called Aspergillus niger that contains an enzyme (Alpha-Galactosidase) that will break down oligosaccharides, preventing your large intestinal bacteria from creating gas. You can buy it at stores everywhere under the auspicious name "Beano." If you don't want to be seen sprinkling your beans with this product, you can always try soaking your beans in water for several hours before you make your food. This softens the beans and allows them to ferment. The yeast produced can consume the offending oligosaccharides and help leave your dinner date vapor-free!

WHY HAIR ONLY GROWS TO A CERTAIN LENGTH

Hair length is completely controlled by the length of the anagen phase of your hair follicle. How long this phase lasts is determined mostly by genetics, but it can also be affected by hormones and extreme stress. But in the end, there is a chemical signal that ultimately controls the exact growth cycle.

Following the anagen phase is the catagen phase. It isn't yet known what triggers the catagen phase, but once it is triggered, the outer part of the root is cut off from its nutrient supply (blood), as well as the cells that produce new hair, thus your hair stops growing. This phase lasts about three weeks.

Next up comes the telogen phase where the follicle is in a resting state and your hair is now a "club hair," completely dead down to the root. During this stage, these hairs are relatively easy to pull out (as can happen while brushing/combing/washing your hair), but if they manage to last long enough, they'll eventually be pushed out by a new hair as the cycle begins again.

Obviously hairs on your arms or legs have a very different anagen period than hairs on your head, thus why your leg hair doesn't grow two feet long without trimming. Further, different people, thanks mostly to their genetics, have differing lengths of the anagen period for a given body part compared to other people. For the hair on your head, the average length of the anagen phase is about 2-7 years. For your arms, legs, eyebrows, etc., this phase usually lasts just 30-45 days. However, in extreme cases which are quite rare, some people have anagen periods for their heads as short as most people's anagen phases for their arms and legs. For these people, their hair never naturally grows more than a few inches long. The opposite is also true for people whose anagen phase can last decades for their scalp hair.

At any given time about 85 to 90 percent of your hair is in the anagen phase, 1 to 2 percent is in the catagen phase, and 10 to 14 percent is in the telogen phase. However, extreme stress can trigger the anagen phase to stop prematurely and hair can rapidly progress to the telogen phase, even as much as 70% of the hair on your body. When this happens, the majority of your hair that should still be growing can fall out all at once.

Under normal circumstances, though, you can get a rough estimate of how long your anagen phase is based on how long your hair grows naturally without cutting off a given area. First, assuming your hair isn't already as long as it can get, measure your hair length, then exactly a month later measure it again and note the difference. Now you have your growth rate (usually about 1 centimeter every 28 days or 1 inch every 71 days). So if, without cutting, the hair on your head eventually grows 16 inches long max, then your anagen phase lasts: (inches*period per inch). So using the average of 1 inch every 71 days, (16 inches * 71 days/inch) = approximately 1,136 days or 3.11 years.

As to why when you cut hair, it will always grow back to its maximum length, this is just because when the cycle restarts, new hair comes in that can grow to the maximum length, eventually replacing the old hair that will be shorter than it could have been because you cut it.

As you might have guessed from the fact that hair growth is completely controlled by what's going on under the surface, within your hair follicles, and that genetics and hormones are the primary things determining hair growth length, which are in no way affected by shaving, shaving does not in any way alter your hair growth rate, nor does it alter the color of the hair, contrary to popular belief.

WHY RICE KRISPIES "SNAP, CRACKLE, AND POP"

The popping is a result of the walls of the Rice Krispies kernels fracturing. There are two prevalent theories as to the exact process that results in this fracturing, and it's entirely possible that both are occurring.

Rice Krispies, also known as "Rice Bubbles," in some countries, are created by preparing rice in such a way that it will "pop" like popcorn during the cooking process, albeit much less dramatically. This popping puffs up the kernels. When the rice is finished cooking, most of the Rice Krispies will have thin solid walls with hollow, sealed, areas inside where air pockets have formed.

In the first theory of what causes the fracturing of the walls, the sudden temperature shift caused by adding cold milk to the Rice Krispies causes the air inside the hollow pockets to contract suddenly, which, in turn, fractures the thin walls of the Rice Krispies, creating the noises.

The second theory also involves the fracturing of the thin walls, but by a different mechanism. The thin walls of the Rice Krispies have very strong bonds between the starch molecules due to the high heat the Rice Krispies were prepared at. When you add cold milk, the sudden shift of temperature puts a high amount of stress on these bonds, due to uneven absorption. This is actually the exact same thing that happens when you pour hot water over a frozen windshield. This dramatic temperature shift causes both the glass in the windshield and the walls of the Rice Krispies to shatter.

BONUS FACT

While Rice Krispies are puffed by preparing the kernels with steam to provide the necessary moisture to the kernels to properly "pop" them, other methods to puff up rice, corn, wheat, etc. are also possible. The most popular alternative method is called "gun puffing." In this method, the kernels are cooked under high pressure. When the cooking process is at just the right stage, given the particular kernel, the pressure is released, causing the kernel to rapidly expand. This method tends to produce a spongier end product, rather than a crispy one, like the method used with Rice Krispies.

WHY YOUR NOSE RUNS WHEN IT IS COLD OUTSIDE

On an average day, a typical person's nose will produce about one quart of mucus/fluid (just under one liter). Most all of this snot generally gets passed back into your throat and swallowed, often without you even really being conscious of it. When you're breathing cold air though, the rate of mucus production goes up significantly, causing some of that snot to come out the front of your nose, rather than back in your throat.

What's going on here is the blood supply to your nose increases as a response to the cold air, via tiny blood vessels in your nose dilating to increase the blood flow. This helps keep your nose warm as you breathe, as well as begins to warm the cold air you're breathing before it enters your lungs.

This increased blood flow doesn't just help warm the air though, it also has a side effect of providing a lot more blood than normal to the glands that produce the mucus in your nose. This, in turn, causes them to start producing snot at a much higher rate than normal, which causes your nose to run when you're breathing the cold air.

Once you're back in a warm air environment, the blood vessels in your nose will constrict and the glands that produce the mucus/liquid mix will go back to their normal rate of around four cups of snot per day.

BONUS FACT

Your nose runs when you cry because the tears from the tear glands under your eyelids drain into your nose, where they mix with mucus to form very liquidy snot.

WHY A DOLLAR IS CALLED A "BUCK"

As with many etymologies, the exact root of this word is difficult to say with one hundred percent certainty. However, the leading theory is extremely plausible and backed up by a fair bit of documented evidence. Specifically, it is thought that a dollar is called a "buck" thanks to deer.

One of the earliest references of this was in 1748, about 44 years before the first U.S. dollar was minted, where there is a reference to the exchange rate for a cask of whiskey traded to Native Americans being "5 bucks", referring to deerskins.

In yet another documented reference from 1748, Conrad Weiser, while traveling through present day Ohio, noted in his journal that someone had been "robbed of the value of 300 Bucks."

At this time, a buck skin was a common medium of exchange. There is also evidence that a "buck" didn't simply mean one deerskin, but may have meant multiple skins, depending on quality. For instance, skins from deer killed in the winter were considered superior to those killed in the summer, due to the fur being thicker.

It is thought that the highest quality skins were generally assigned a one to one value with one skin equaling one buck. In contrast, for lower quality skins, it might take several of them to be valued at a single buck. The specific value for given sets of skins was then set at trading.

In addition, when the skin was from another animal, the number of skins required to equal a buck varied based on the animal and the quality of the skins. For instance, there is one documented trade where six high quality beaver skins or twelve high quality rabbit pelts each equaled one buck.

This use of skins as a medium of exchange gradually died off over the next century as more and more Europeans moved in and built towns and cities. Once the U.S. dollar was officially introduced after the passing of the Coinage Act of 1792, it quickly became the leading item used as a medium of exchange, but the term "buck" stuck around and by the mid-nineteenth century was being used as a slang term for the dollar.

BONUS FACT

While it may be tempting to think that the "buck" in this sense is where we also get the phrase "pass the buck", most etymologists don't think the two are related. The leading theory on the origin of the phrase "pass the buck" is thought to come from poker, with one of the earliest known references of the idea of literally passing a buck being found in the 1887 work by J.W. Keller, titled "Draw Poker". In it, Keller states:

"The 'buck' is any inanimate object, usually knife or pencil, which is thrown into a jack pot and temporarily taken by the winner of the pot. Whenever the deal reaches the holder of the 'buck,' a new jack pot must be made."

As to why it is then called a buck, it is thought that may have arisen from the fact that buck-handled knives were once common and knives were often used as the "buck" in this sense. As for the figurative sense of passing the buck, this didn't start popping up until the early twentieth century.

WHY IT'S TRADITIONAL TO CHRISTEN A SHIP BY SMASHING A BOTTLE OF CHAMPAGNE AGAINST THE HULL

While today breaking a bottle of champagne over the hull of a ship is considered tradition before launching a vessel in certain countries, particularly Britain and the United States, people have been performing ceremonies at launches seemingly as long as humans have made boats.

Like today, this was essentially for the hope of good fortune on the ship's voyages. For instance, one of the earliest known references to a similar practice when launching a ship goes all the way back about 5,000 years ago when a Babylonian stated, "To the gods I caused oxen to be sacrificed," before launching a new ship he'd made.

The ancient Greeks, Romans, and Egyptians also called upon their various gods to protect a new ship and her crew upon its initial launch. For example, the ancient Greeks, during their launch festivities, would drink wine to honor the gods and pour water on the ship as a sort of blessing.

The religious aspects of ship christening remained well into more modern times, particularly in Catholic nations. For example, there's an account of a ship christening by the Knights of Malta in the seventeenth century that describes two friars boarding a new warship, praying, and sprinkling holy water all around the ship before deeming her seaworthy and sending her out into the water.

After the Protestant Reformation, kicking off in earnest after Martin Luther's 1517 "Ninety-Five Thesis", certain nations in Europe did away with some aspects of the religious part of the christening. Rather than use religious leaders for this task, members of the monarchy or military leaders would take over the christening duties.

For instance, 65 years before the above Knights of Malta reference, in 1610, the Prince of Wales was present at the christening of the Prince Royal. In this instance, there was a standing cup on board the ship, which is just a large and expensive cup made of some precious metal, usually silver. The Prince took a ceremonial sip of the wine in the cup before throwing the rest of the contents across the deck. The cup was then thrown off the side of the ship to be caught by a lucky observer.

Late in the seventeenth century, the standing cup ceremony was replaced with breaking a bottle of wine over the bow. This switch was in part because the cups were extremely valuable and the British navy was growing rapidly; it just wasn't practical to continue to give the expensive cups away every time a ship was launched.

As for the switch from wine to champagne, it's thought that preferences simply switched with the times. Champagne came to be seen as an "aristocratic" choice -for a time in the nineteenth century being more popular than wine among many elite –and, therefore, considered the best option for ship christening. The tradition of using it has stuck around ever since in certain countries.

BONUS FACT

Rather than use champagne to christen new ships, in Japan, it's traditional to have a special silver axe made with the axe being used to cut the lines holding the ship from plunging into the water. After the cutting ceremony, the axe is usually kept by the ship's owner.

WHY COUPONS SOMETIMES SAY THEY ARE WORTH A FRACTION OF A PENNY

Depending on where you live, you may have noticed that coupons have small print stating they are worth some fraction of a penny, usually something like 1/100th or 1/20th of a penny.

In truth, the coupons really are worth this and if you wanted, you could redeem them for their cash value. Of course, you'd need a large quantity of them to even reach a penny's worth. The price goes up even more if you're interested in making a profit as you'll often need to mail the coupons in to redeem the value, depending on the company issuing the coupon.

So why are they worth anything at all? This stems back to the days of trading stamp collecting. For those not familiar, the trading stamp system was a fairly brilliant customer loyalty program used by various businesses starting around the 1890s in the United States and later spreading to other countries. In exchange for spending some dollar amount, a business would give out otherwise worthless stamps and stamp books that they had purchased from certain stamp companies. The more you spent, the more stamps you'd get.

Humans are a funny lot and even if nothing else was given, this collecting system would have had a tangible effect on customer loyalty. But to up the incentive for caring about how many stamps you acquired, you could trade in your stamps to the stamp companies for various "freebies," depending on how many stamps you had. In the early days, discounts on gasoline were an extremely popular "freebie" with customers, as with many customer loyalty programs today.

This wasn't costing businesses much of anything as they, of course, incorporated the cost of the stamps into the prices they were selling their products for. Further, you'd have to collect a pretty large amount of stamps to get anything of real value. For instance, an article in a 1904 edition of the *New York Times* indicated that you'd typically get about 1/3 of a penny per stamp (about 8.33 cents today), in terms of the price of the thing you traded your stamps for.

How much would you have to spend to acquire a stamp at this

time? This varied from company to company, but in general you could expect to spend 10 cents per stamp (about $2.52 today).

Eventually, the fact that trading stamps had no set dollar value, other than perhaps the miniscule value of the raw material the stamps were printed on -essentially nothing then -led to legislation in the early twentieth century requiring that the stamps themselves be given some monetary value. This way, if customers chose, instead of trading them in for some product, they could simply cash them in for money.

Limits were set on the minimum value allowed per stamp, and most trading stamp companies went ahead and assigned that value to their stamps to keep people opting for trading in stamps for products, that these companies bought in bulk at a great discount from the retail prices. This minimum cash value was around 1/3 to 1/4 what you could usually get for trading the stamps in for some product, so exceptionally few people traded the stamps in for money.

What does this have to do with coupons? In certain regions, the law governing the old trading stamp system also applies to physical coupons given to customers. Thus, in those regions, coupons also need to have some monetary value.

Today, the *Association of Coupon Professionals* claims that in the United States only three states still require a monetary value be given to coupons: Washington, Indiana, and Utah. However, as many large business chains don't want to print different coupons for different regions -and knowing that almost no one is going to bother to try to cash the coupons in for their monetary value -they simply give coupons a tiny monetary value based on the minimum limit they can get away with.

BONUS FACT

By the 1960s, one of the top trading stamp companies, S&H Green Stamps, was boasting that they printed more stamps annually than the U.S. Postal Service. At this time, an estimated 80% of the people in the U.S. actively collected various brands of trading stamps (of which there were many). However, within a decade the trading stamp boom would decline abruptly, with most businesses choosing at that point to develop their own customer loyalty programs and specifically to divert the money they were spending on trading stamps to lowering product prices, often by issuing coupons for direct money off purchased items, as well as advertising their sales.

WHY PROPER STERLIZATION PROCEDURES ARE USED DURING LETHAL INJECTIONS

Besides the fact that manufacturers sterilize the needles (so no real extra effort is needed), other sterilization procedures are also used in these executions for good reason.

You see, a stay of execution may happen at the last minute. If this happens, but then the condemned later dies from infection from the needle, a wrongful death suit could be filed against the state -a suit the state would likely lose.

While this may seem like a scenario that is unlikely to occur in real life, in fact, this is not the case at all. Relatively last minute granting of a stay of execution is incredibly common, though ones where the needle is already inserted are rare.

That being said, it has happened before. Exhibit A: James David Autry. Autry was convicted of murdering convenience store employee Shirley Drouet and customer Joe Broussard, who was in the store at the time. Another customer in the store was Anthanasios Svarnas, who was shot, but not killed. What did Autry get out of this? Some beer worth $2.70 (about $7.41 today); he didn't take any money from the cash register, just the beer.

About three years after the murders, on October 4, 1983, Autry found himself strapped down with a needle in his arm, about to be injected with a concoction of chemicals that would end his life. However, at the time, there was a question whether Texas' exact procedure for executions was constitutional.

After lying there for a little over a half hour, the call came in. The Supreme Court had ruled that Autry's execution be delayed for 30 days while they continued to review the issue. The needle was removed and Autry was taken back to his cell.

Of course, five months later, on March 14, 1984, he was executed. But in the interim, had they not used proper sterilization procedures, he may well have gotten sick or even died as a result. It's considered okay for some states to kill condemned prisoners in a properly vetted procedure, but not via infection.

Yet another ultra-close call case is that of Warren Lee Hill, a man with the IQ of just 70. Hill received a life sentence for murdering his girlfriend in 1985. Five years later, he beat another inmate, Joseph Handspike, to death and was given the death penalty. In July of 2012, just a few hours before he was to be executed, he was given a stay of execution. Later, on February 19, 2013, he was once again to be executed -this time, a stay of execution was granted a scant 30 minutes before he was to have the lethal concoction of chemicals course through his veins. To date, he has received four stays of executions and as of the publication of this book (December, 2013), he hasn't been executed yet.

In as close of a call as you can get -though this time the individual was not subject to lethal injection -Caryl Chessman was given a stay of execution so near to the set execution time that it ended up being too late. In 1948, Chessman, who'd robbed various people and raped several women, was sentenced to die via the gas chamber. After garnering support from the likes of Billy Graham and Eleanor Roosevelt, he was granted eight stays of execution.

The problem was, in the last one, it occurred about one minute before the execution was to take place. The secretary of the federal judge who'd granted the stay accidentally dialed the wrong number. By the time she realized her mistake and called the correct number, the cyanide pellets had been dropped. At this point, there was nothing that could be done to stop the execution, and Chessman died.

BONUS FACT

The general lethal injection procedure usually employed by most prisons involves first introducing a saline drip, then injecting the condemned with a general anesthesia, hopefully which won't have worn off before the fatal fluids have done their work. Once the condemned is unconscious, some chemical is used to cause death via cardiac arrest. To achieve this, usually Pancuronium bromide is injected, resulting in the individual ceasing breathing. After the Pancuronium bromide is introduced, Potassium chloride comes next, which stops the heart.

WHY WHEN WE WANT SOMETHING DONE QUICKLY WE SAY "STAT"

This may seem odd at first glance. After all, common usage of "stat" outside of these instances is referring to statistics. In this case, though, "stat" is not short for "statistics," but rather is from the Latin "statim," meaning "immediately" or "at once." The first references of the practice of shortening "statim" to "stat" came to us from physicians in the nineteenth century, with the first known documented instance of this appearing in *Lessons on Prescriptions* by W.H. Griffith (1875).

BONUS FACT

"Wiki" as used in "Wikipedia," means "quick." Howard G. Cunningham, the developer of the first wiki which was launched in 1995 called "WikiWikiWeb," upon his first visit to Hawaii was informed by an airport employee that he needed to take the "wiki wiki" bus between the airport's terminals. Not understanding what the person was telling him, he inquired further and found out "wiki" means "quick" in Hawaiian; by repeating the word, it gives additional emphasis and thus means "very quick." He later decided to use this as the name for his new web platform.

The shorter version of the name, calling a wiki just "wiki" instead of "Wiki Wiki" came about because Cunningham's first implementation of WikiWikiWeb named the original cgi script "wiki" -all lower case and abbreviated in the standard Unix fashion. Thus, the first wiki url was http://c2.com/cgi/wiki. People latched onto this and simply called it a "wiki" instead of a "Wiki Wiki."

It should also be noted that the proper pronunciation of "wiki" is technically "we-key", rather than "wick-ee". However, given the popularity of the mispronunciation of the word, Cunningham and others have long since stopped trying to correct people on the matter.

WHY "POINDEXTER" IS SLANG FOR "NERD"

"Poindexter" as a slang name for a nerdy person comes from a particularly memorable stereotypically nerdy character in the cartoon *Felix the Cat*. The character in question is the nephew of Felix's archenemy, the Professor, who is, of course, named Poindexter.

Poindexter was first introduced to the masses in 1959 in the cartoon version of *Felix the Cat* shown on TV. Over the years, he has typically been depicted in a lab coat, wearing thick glasses, and otherwise personifying stereotypical nerdom in all its glory.

Despite having been around for decades, it took another Hollywood creation to really get the popularity of this slang term firmly implanted into common vernacular, rather than as a fringe moniker for nerds. This occurred in the mid-1980s thanks to the character of Arnold Poindexter in the 1984 *Revenge of the Nerds*. Since then, "Poindexter" has been a relatively popular moniker for anyone who exhibits extremely nerdy tendencies.

BONUS FACT

The first documented case of "nerd" was in Dr. Seuss's *If I Ran the Zoo*, in 1950. The specific text was: "a Nerkle, a Nerd, and a Seersucker too." It was just one year after this Dr. Seuss work that, in a *Newsweek* magazine article, we find the first documented case of "nerd" being used similarly to how we use it today. Specifically, they used it as being synonymous with someone who was a "drip" or a "square."

As to how exactly "nerd" came to mean as we think of it today, the most popular theory -by no means certain -is that it came from a modification of "nut," specifically "nert," which meant "stupid or crazy person," and was common in the 1940s, directly before the term "nerd" showed up. The word "nerd" became fairly popular in the 1960s and by the 1970s was hugely popularized by the TV show *Happy Days*, where it was used frequently.

You might also at this point be wondering about the origin of "geek." The first documented case of "geek" dates all the way back to 1916. At the time, the term was used to describe sideshow freaks in circuses. Specifically, it was typically attributed to those circus performers who were known for doing crazy things like biting the heads of various small live animals or eating live insects and the like. These performances were often called "geek shows." The word itself, "geek," came from "geck," which was originally a Low German word meaning someone who is a "fool / freak / simpleton."

WHY ENGINES ARE COMMONLY MEASURED IN HORSEPOWER

We owe this unit of engine power measurement to Scottish engineer James Watt.

In the early 1780s, after making a vastly superior steam engine to the then classic Newcomen steam engine, Watt was looking for a way to market his invention, advertising the fact that his engine used about 75% less fuel than a similarly powered Newcomen, among many other improvements.

At first, he tried selling his engine on a royalty scheme, where the customers would owe him one-third of the money they saved by using his engine over other steam engines. Of course, many at the time used horses, not steam engines, so it was difficult to compare without them actually buying the engine to see how it would perform for their particular usage. Thus, he scrapped the royalty scheme and decided to try a different tact to convince people to buy his engine.

Ever the inventor, his solution was to come up with a new unit of measurement that those in need of his engine understood -horse power, referring to powerful draft horses.

Thus, he set about determining how much power a typical draft horse could generate. It isn't known exactly how he came up with the numbers he did, as there are conflicting accounts of the experiments he ran. But after doing those experiments, he figured out a typical draft horse could do about 32,400 foot-pounds of work in 60 seconds and maintain that power rate for a good long workday. He then rounded up, going with 33,000 foot-pounds per minute for 1 horsepower.

So, in other words, by his estimation a good draft horse could lift 33,000 pounds of material 1 foot in 1 minute or 3,300 pounds of material 10 feet in one minute, etc .

In truth, that's a very generous estimate as very few horses could maintain that kind of power for a full workday, but getting a perfect figure wasn't that important to what Watt was trying to do. Further, by overestimating what a horse could do, whether intentionally or not, he made sure that his product would always over deliver what he said when trying to get people to buy it, which is a great word-of-mouth marketing trick.

In the end, Watt's engine was revolutionary and played a huge role in the Industrial Revolution. Thanks to this fact, his unit of measure of an engine's power, horsepower, also became popular. Funny enough, today the SI unit of power, the Watt, which was named in homage to James Watt, has widely come to replace "horsepower" in most applications.

BONUS FACT

While Watt came up with the exact measurement of what would become "horsepower," he was not the first to propose the idea of equating a steam engine's power to a horse's. The first documented instance of this was suggested by British inventor Thomas Savery who wrote the following in a letter in 1702: "So that an engine which will raise as much water as two horses, working together at one time in such a work, can do, and for which there must be constantly kept ten or twelve horses for doing the same. Then I say, such an engine may be made large enough to do the work required in employing eight, ten, fifteen, or twenty horses to be constantly maintained and kept for doing such a work..."

WHY SIDEBURNS ARE NAMED "SIDEBURNS"

Despite this particular brand of facial hair style being around as far back as at least 100 BC, with one of the earliest known instances being in a Roman floor mosaic of Alexander the Great who lived from 356 BC to 323 BC (with the mosaic possibly being a copy of a painting from Alexander's era), sideburns were named after a specific man in the late nineteenth century.

Ambrose Burnside was a politician, businessman, and Union Army General. Burnside sported a slightly unusual facial hair style with particularly prominent "mutton chop" sideburns connected to a moustache, while keeping his chin shaved perfectly clean.

While an extremely poor General, something he himself was well aware of, Burnside's popularity as a General and later politician, in combination with the fairly unique formation of his whiskers, helped start something of a new facial hair trend. Around the 1870s-1880s, this gave rise to this facial hair style being named "burnsides."

Within a few years of this, the facial hair down the side of one's cheeks, rather than being called "mutton chops" as it was at the time in some regions, began being called a modification of "burnsides," "sideburns," with the first documented instance of this being in 1887. Presumably the shift was from the fact that this part of the "burnsides" facial hair style was on the sides of the face and, of course, leaving the "burns" part in homage to the aforementioned style.

BONUS FACT

The English word "moustache" comes from the French word of the same spelling, "moustache," and popped up in English around the sixteenth century. The French word comes from the Italian word "mostaccio," from the Medieval Latin "mustacium" and, in turn, the Medieval Greek "moustakion." We now finally get to the earliest known origin, the Hellenistic Greek "mustax," meaning "upper lip," which may or may not have come from the Hellenistic Greek "mullon," meaning "lip." It is theorized that this came from the Proto-Indo-European root "*mendh-", meaning "to chew" (which is also where we get the word "mandible").

WHY CHEMOTHERAPY CAUSES HAIR TO FALL OUT

This has to do with how different types of chemotherapy target cancer cells. There are many different chemotherapy drugs that work in a variety of ways, so I will only speak in general terms regarding their side effects.

Most cells in the human body divide using a process called mitosis. This process has five phases (prophase, prometaphase, metaphase, anaphase, and telephase). It is preceded by interphase, and results in the cell dividing, called cytokinesis. When a cell reaches the end of its lifespan, it gets destroyed in a pre-programed process called apoptosis.

There are many types of cancer (over 200). All types are a result of the same problem -unregulated cell growth. The result is excessive tissue, known as tumors. These tumors can be localized, or they can spread to surrounding areas through your lymphatic system or your blood stream.

Many chemotherapy drugs work by interrupting mitosis. Most chemotherapy cannot differentiate between abnormal cancer cells and normal healthy cells. Because of this, cells that have high mitotic rates (multiply rapidly) can also be affected by chemotherapy, cells like those found in your hair follicles, the lining of your mouth and stomach, and those found in your bone marrow.

The result can be hair loss, decrease in production of white blood cells (thus why cancer patients are immune-suppressed), and inflammation of your digestive tract. In the end, chemotherapy will hopefully kill the cancer cells, and in the process, unfortunately, potentially cause hair loss. However, the healthy cells of one's hair follicles will repair themselves, making hair loss temporary, as is hopefully the cancer!

BONUS FACT

Normal healthy cells divide and die as they should. This leads one to ask, "How many times"? The average number of times normal healthy cells divide is known as the Hayflick Limit. It was named after Dr. Leonard Hayflick, who in 1965 noticed that cells divide a specific number of times before the division stops. The average is between 40 and 60 times.

If you took every cell in your body at the time you were born and accounted for all the cells they would produce and so on, then multiplied that number by the average time it takes for those cells to die, you get what is known as the Ultimate Hayflick Limit. The maximum number of years you can theoretically live. That would be about 120 years!

That being said, a significant amount of research is being done to find ways around this, with some promising results, such as using a ribonucleoprotein called "telomerase." In a nutshell, when introduced, telomerase allows dividing cells to replace lost bits of DNA information, allowing cell division to continue, in theory, forever. While this hasn't been proven, it has been shown to allow for cell division far beyond the Hayflick limit.

WHY BLUEPRINTS ARE BLUE

Making copies of architectural drawings hasn't always been the easiest thing to do in the world. For the majority of human history, the most economical solution was simply to have someone make a tracing of the original plans.

In the mid-nineteenth century, the process abruptly became much quicker and easier thanks to famed polymath Sir John Herschel. In 1842, Herschel invented a method to easily copy drawings using potassium ferrocyanide and ammonium iron citrate.

The exact method, called cyanotype, is performed as follows. First, you take a drawing of the plans done on relatively translucent tracing paper or cloth and place it on top of and attach it to paper (or sometimes linen, Mylar, etc.) that has been previously soaked in a mixture of the aforementioned two chemicals, then dried. Next, you expose the papers to a bright ultra-violet light source, such as the Sun, for several minutes.

The result is that the paper soaked in the chemicals ends up turning blue as the chemicals react to the light and form a compound called blue ferric ferrocyanide, also known as "Prussian Blue."

This wouldn't be very helpful for making a copy of a document except for the fact that where the light cannot penetrate the translucent paper, namely where the drawing marks are, the coated paper remains the original color of the paper, usually white, effectively making a nice copy.

You might see a potential problem here in that you then can't expose the un-blued bits to any bright light source at first, but this problem is easily solved by simply washing the chemicals off, then allowing the paper to dry. At this point, the copy is complete.

Within a few decades of the discovery of this method of copying (as well as other blue-printing methods such as one developed by Alphonse Louis Poitevin in 1861 using ferro-gallate), the price dropped to about one-tenth the cost of having someone simply trace the original plans, helping the popularity of blueprints explode.

In the mid-twentieth century, copying methods such as as diazo prints, and then later xerographic prints, finally supplanted blueprints. Much more recently, simply sticking with digital versions of plans has become popular, with these having the advantage of being easy to modify and distribute as needed during the construction process.

Despite the technological changes and the fact that these plans usually aren't on blue paper anymore, in popular vernacular the term "blueprints" has stuck around anyways.

BONUS FACT

Besides contributing the cyanotype blueprinting method to the world, Sir John Herschel was also the first to apply the terms "negative" and "positive" to photography; named seven of the moons of Saturn; did a translation of *The Iliad* into English; greatly influenced Charles Darwin's work, with Darwin calling Herschel "one of our greatest philosophers" in *On the Origin of Species*; among many, many other contributions to various fields, particularly astronomy, as well as the emerging field of photography.

WHY SUPERHEROES WEAR THEIR UNDERWEAR ON THE OUTSIDE

While there have been many fantastical proposed origins of this seemingly odd modish style amongst comic artists -my favorite of which being that most superheroes lost their parents at an early age, so they had no one to tell them underwear goes UNDER your clothes -the true origin is pretty simple. According to Julius Schwartz (famed editor of DC Comics from 1944-1986 who edited the most famous of all external-underwear superheroes, Superman), this was simply modeled after the garb of aerial circus performers and wrestlers of the era in which the first superheroes proudly donned their underpants over their tights.

Now, it should be noted here that the wrestlers, circus performers, and superheroes weren't actually wearing underwear, but rather tight underwear-like shorts over their leggings. As superheroes are generally incredibly gifted athletically and perform amazing acrobatic stunts while crime fighting, it was natural enough for this style of dress to get adopted by the earliest superhero artists for their characters.

Two of the earliest major representations of this can be found in *Flash Gordon* (1934), which in turn was partially the inspiration for the garb of *Superman* (1938), with the principle difference being the colors of their uniforms and the fact that Superman had a cape (as far as I can find, the first major superhero to wear one).

Of course, if you still want to think of the superhero tight-shorts as underwear, given that Superman and others often wear their uniform under their normal clothes, it kind of makes sense.

BONUS FACT

The original Superman character envisioned by Jerry Siegal and Joe Shuster was not the crime-fighting hero from another world we know today. Instead, they made him a bald bad guy set on ruling the world in the 1933 *The Reign of Superman*. In this story, a character by the name of Bill Dunn is waiting in a soup kitchen line when Professor Ernest Smalley offers him food and new clothes in exchange for his participation in an experiment. The Professor proceeds to give him a potion that makes Dunn telepathic; he then becomes a super-man, and tries to take over the world. However, in the process, he kills Professor Smalley, only to discover later that his powers are temporary unless he has more potion to drink, which he can't figure out how to recreate. Ultimately, the former Superman finds himself without his powers and back in the soup kitchen line.

A year after writing that story, Siegel re-cast the character of Superman, this time making him a hero bent on righting the wrongs prominent in society at the time. They also decided to switch Superman's name from "Bill Dunn" to "Clark Kent," after famed actors Kent Taylor and Clark Gable.

WHY POLICE OFFICERS ARE SOMETIMES CALLED "PIGS"

Unlike so many other nicknames for the police, such as cops, peelers, and the fuzz, this particular term has a relatively well known origin. You see, starting around the sixteenth century "pig" began being used in English as a derogatory term for people, whether police or not, as it still sometimes is used today. It took about three more centuries, but this particular insult inevitably became a popular nickname for oft-insulted police officers, with the first documented reference to this being in the *Dictionary of Buckish Slang, University Wit and Pickpocket Eloquence*, published in London in 1811.

In it, the pertinent line in question is: "The pigs frisked my panney, and nailed my screws." Meaning: "The officers searched my house, and seized my picklocks."

BONUS FACT

"Bobbies" are named after former British Prime Minister, Sir Robert Peel, who helped revolutionize the British police force. The less commonly known "peelers" nickname also comes from Sir Robert.

As for other common nicknames for the police, we have to delve into murkier waters, but "cop" probably came from "copper" / "to cop," meaning "capture" or "seize," possibly originally derived from the Latin "capere," meaning "to seize," though this isn't known for sure.

As for "the fuzz," this term has no origin story nearly definitive enough for me to mention here, with etymologists mostly just guessing in this instance. Though, for your reference, it first popped up among various criminals in the 1920s in North America.

WHY SOME COUNTRIES DRIVE ON THE RIGHT AND SOME ON THE LEFT

The origin of this practice varies based on the time period and country, but primarily, throughout history, people used the "keep-left" rule. Only very recently did the world predominately switch to "keep-right".

The first real archaeological evidence of a keep-left or keep-right type rule for a road originates in the Roman Empire, which shouldn't be surprising as they built a lot of massive, well-trafficked roads spanning Europe and thus would have needed to establish certain rules governing how people were to interact on the roads.

So which side did the Romans use? Archaeological evidence suggests it was common for the Romans to drive on the left side of the road. One confirmation of this was discovered in 1998 where a Roman quarry in Swindon, England, had grooves in the road going away from the quarry on the left side that were significantly deeper than those on the right, due to the added weight of the stone. It is not precisely known why they would have chosen this side, but it is probably similar to one of the main reasons this practice continued into the Middle Ages.

During the Middle Ages, the roads weren't always very safe for travelers; meeting people coming the other way on the road was something best done defensively. From this, many historians believe the keep-left rule was adopted because, on a horse, if you were right-handed and you met some unsavory company on the road, you could draw your weapon, typically attached to your left side, with your right hand and bring it to bear quickly against the person who is going the opposite way of you on your right; all the while, controlling the reigns with your left hand. Then of course, if you happened to meet a friend on the road, you could more easily offer your right hand in greeting without needing to reach across your body when on horseback. Back then, people on horseback typically ruled the road, so everybody else followed suit.

This keep-left rule was so common that in 1300 AD Pope Boniface VIII decreed that all pilgrims headed to Rome, from wherever they were coming from, should abide by the keep-left rule of the road along their journey. This held across most of the

Western World until the late 1700s.

The switch to the keep-right rule occurred in the eighteenth century when teamsters in the United States would drive large wagons with a team of horses, as the name implies. These wagons tended to dominate the streets and forced everybody else to abide by the rule of the road the teamsters were using. Very importantly, in many of those old, large American wagons, they did not include a seat on the wagon for the driver. Rather, the driver would typically sit on the rear left most horse, when the driver was right-handed. This allowed him to easily drive a whole team of horses with a lash in his right hand.

This forced the issue of having oncoming traffic on your left as the drivers would want to make sure that no part of their team or wagon collided with oncoming traffic. When sitting on the rear left-most horse, this was much easier to do when using a keep-right rule of the road.

Gradually, this system spread so that by the late eighteenth century, the first laws concerning this in the United States were passed, starting in 1792 in Pennsylvania, where the rule of the road was now officially a keep-right rule. This quickly spread throughout the United States and Canada.

So how did this spread through Europe? It started with France. The reasons why the French switched to a keep-right rule instead of the traditional keep-left rule aren't completely clear. Some say it is because the French Revolutionists didn't want anything to do with something that a Pope had decreed. Others say it was because they didn't want to use the same rule of the road the English used. Still others say it was entirely Napoleon's doing. The reasons why he may have done this, if that is the case, are even more a matter of pure speculation.

Whatever the real reason, France switched to the keep-right system. Napoleon spread this system throughout the countries he conquered. Even after he was defeated, most of the countries he had conquered chose to continue with the keep-right system.

The most important of these countries, as far as eventually further spreading the keep-right system, was Germany. Fast forward to the twentieth century and, as Germany conquered countries in Europe, they forced their keep-right system onto those countries.

England never adopted this method primarily because massive

wagons, as became common in the United States, didn't work well on narrow streets, which were common in London and other major English cities. England was also never conquered by Napoleon or later Germany. Thus, they kept the classic keep-left rule of the road that had endured for hundreds of years before. By 1756, this "keep left" rule was made an official law in Britain, originally referring to protocols when traveling over the London Bridge.

As the British Empire expanded, this keep-left rule, as a law, also spread somewhat. This hasn't endured in most of the former British ruled countries, primarily thanks to Germany and the growing popularity of the keep-right system. There are still a few holdouts though, probably the largest of which, by population, is India. Although, if you've ever driven in most regions of India, you'll know that any supposed "rules" of the road are more just extremely loosely followed guidelines.

WHY EATING ASPARAGUS MAKES YOUR PEE SMELL

The smell comes from the way certain chemical compounds in asparagus break down inside people's bodies. This is why cooking asparagus in various ways does not result in the same smelly by-product; the specific digestive enzymes that break down the compounds in the asparagus to produce the smell aren't present until you eat the asparagus.

As to this specific resulting chemical compound that ends up causing the smell, it has long been thought that it is from methanethiol. Methanethiol is a colorless gas that smells a bit like rotting cabbage. It is composed primarily of sulfur, but also includes hydrogen and carbon.

More recent research by Robert H. White from the University of California proposes an alternative theory. White used gas chromatography-mass spectrometry to try to identify the cause of the smell and he concluded that it was actually from the s-methyl thioesters, specifically s-methyl thioacrylate and s-methyl thiopropionate. Thioesters, like methanethiol, are primarily sulfur based except they are formed from sulfur bonding with an acyl group.

In either case, the ability of a particular person to produce the necessary smelly compound in their urine after digesting asparagus was thought to be a genetic trait unique to only some humans until relatively recently. Recent research done in France, China, and Israel, all independently showed this is not the case. Rather, all humans appear to produce the smelly compound, but only some humans can detect the smell; the ability to detect the smell or not is a genetic trait. Further, according to the study done in Israel, only about 22% of people have that genetic ability to smell the odor from the urine of people who have recently eaten asparagus.

WHY MULTIVITAMINS OFTEN MAKE URINE BRIGHT YELLOW

If you've ever taken a daily multivitamin you might have noticed your urine turning a bright yellow-ish color. Take your vitamins and eat some asparagus and you might just think you're dying the next time you pee!

What's happening is that urine will turn a bright, sometimes neon, yellow in response to excess riboflavin.

Riboflavin, also known as vitamin B2, is a common ingredient in almost all multi-vitamins. It was first discovered in 1872 when chemist Alexander Wynter Blyth noticed a pigment in milk that was yellow-green.

In 1879, it was reported as lactochrome and lactoflavin. It wasn't until the 1930s that the substance giving off a yellow pigment was characterized as riboflavin. (The "flavin" portion coming from the Latin word "flavus," meaning "yellow" or "blonde.")

So why does riboflavin give off a yellowish color? Like almost anything that has color, it all comes down to light absorption.

Light, in general, is merely electromagnetic radiation. This radiation comes to us in a waveform and is classified by its wavelength. Shorter wavelengths come to us in the form of x-rays and ultraviolet light. Longer wavelengths come to us in the form of things like microwaves and radio waves. The light we can see is actually only a very narrow band of wavelength between 400-700 nanometers in length. The color is classified by the length. For example, 400-500 nanometers will appear blue, and 600-700 nanometers will appear red.

The colors we see are a result of the wavelengths not absorbed by the material. So if a material absorbs light in the 400-500 nanometers range (blue) then the color we will perceive is in the 500-700 nanometers range (greens, yellows and reds).

Riboflavin absorbs light strongly in the 260-370 nanometers range. While this falls outside of the light we can see with our eyes, it's also Riboflavin's ability to absorb light at 450 nanometers (the blues) that give it its distinctive yellowish color.

So why does it turn pee yellow? The answer is simply how the body gets rid of excess.

Approximately 50% of all excess riboflavin introduced to the body gets excreted in urine. Further, the maximum amount that can be absorbed in a single dose is about 27 milligrams, with half of that being absorbed in the first 1.1 hours. Given that the recommended adult daily intake of riboflavin is between 1-1.6 milligrams per day and some common doses of riboflavin in multivitamins (that I could find) are 25, 50, and 100 milligrams, it's easy to see that excess amounts can be easily attained.

When this excess of riboflavin is present, the result is a nice bright yellow color to your urine.

BONUS FACT

The term "vitamin" was first put forth by Kazimierz Funk, a Polish scientist in 1912. It comes from the Latin word "vita" meaning "life," combined with "amine" after certain compounds, such as thiamine (Vitamin B1), which he was able to isolate from rice husks. At the time, he was looking for what it was about brown rice vs. milled rice that made people eating brown rice less susceptible to getting Beriberi, which it turns out is primarily caused by lack of thiamine in one's diet.

WHY AMBULANCES ARE CALLED "AMBULANCES"

The word "ambulance" ultimately derives from the Latin "ambulare," meaning "to walk." This gave rise to the French "hôpital ambulant," essentially meaning "mobile hospital." In the beginning, this didn't mean as we think of it today, but was generally just used to refer to a temporary medical structure that could be easily moved, particularly early on referring to movable army medical hospitals.

"Ambulance," in English, first appeared around 1798, which also referred to these temporary hospital structures at first.

Mobile medical transport vehicles were also being called ambulances in French around this time thanks to Frenchman Dominque-Jean Larrey and his "flying ambulance" (ambulance volantes). These ambulances were designed to get injured soldiers off the battlefield and to medical aid during battle, rather than waiting until the fight was over as was common before.

By the mid-nineteenth century, the word (in English) extended to refer to any vehicle used to transport the wounded from battle fields to the military hospitals. One of the first instances of this was during the Crimean War (1853-1856). Shortly thereafter, during the American Civil War, such medical transport vehicles were known as "ambulance wagons." The former, "ambulance," name for mobile medical vehicles has stuck around ever since.

BONUS FACT

About half a century after mobile medical transport vehicles were first referred to as ambulances in English, the phrase "ambulance chaser" popped up, referring to a certain type of lawyer (first attested around 1897).

WHY IT'S COMMON TO YELL "GERONIMO" WHEN JUMPING OUT OF A PLANE OR FROM A HIGH PLACE

In the 1940s, the U.S. Army was testing out the feasibility of having platoons of soldiers parachute from airplanes rapidly. One of the first units to attempt to group jump out of a plane was located in Fort Benning, Georgia.

According to Major Gerard M. Devlin, they came up with the tradition of yelling Geronimo as follows: On the night before the group was set to make their first group jump, they all got together and went out for a night on the town, including going to see a movie and getting as drunk as possible afterward at a bar.

The movie they saw is reported to have been the 1939 film, *Geronimo*, though that isn't known for sure. What is known was that it was a film featuring a character representing the Apache, Geronimo; so it's assumed it was that film as the dates more or less line up.

In any event, while out carousing after the movie, a certain Private by the name of Aubrey Eberhardt was acting tough about the jump that was to happen the next day, making out that it wasn't a big deal and he wasn't nervous about it.

His fellow soldiers called B.S. on him and one of them reportedly exclaimed, "You'll be so scared, you won't remember your own name!" To which he supposedly replied, "All right, dammit! I tell you jokers what I'm gonna do! To prove to you that I'm not scared out of my wits when I jump, I'm gonna yell 'Geronimo' loud as hell when I go out that door tomorrow!"

This is possibly in reference to the story that the Native American Geronimo was given that name by Mexican soldiers after incidents where Geronimo, showing complete disregard for his own personal safety, attacked armed Mexican soldiers with nothing but a knife, surviving each of those attacks despite being constantly shot at. The name is thought to stem from the soldiers yelling and pleading to Saint Jerome for help as they faced Geronimo.

The next day, right after Eberhardt jumped out of the plane, he kept his promise and yelled at the top of his lungs, "Geronimo!" and added some Native American mimicking war whoops, just for good measure. This tradition of making a ridiculous exclamation as loud as possible in the face of death right after jumping out of a plane (these early paratroopers didn't exactly have the best survival rates) caught on with the rest of Eberhardt's unit and they all began exclaiming, "Geronimo," when they jumped.

Whether Major Devlin's recollection of events is perfectly accurate or not, once training was complete, this practice had become so popular that when the Army christened the 501st Parachute Infantry Battalion in 1941, which was the first combat ready parachute unit, they put "Geronimo" on their insignia and most of the troops would yell it as they jumped from the planes.

This caught on with the general public thanks to extensive news media coverage of these parachuting troops -jumping out of a plane obviously being something of a novelty at the time.

WHY ASSOCIATION FOOTBALL IS CALLED "SOCCER" IN AMERICA

It may surprise you to learn that "Soccer," as a name for "Association Football," was coined by the British. In fact, in the early days of the sport among the upper echelons of British society, the popular name for the sport was "Soccer." Further, the sport being referred to as "Soccer" preceded the first recorded instance of it being called by the singular word "Football" by about 18 years

In the 1860s, as in most of history (with records as far back as 1004 BC where in Japan an Association Football-like sport was played) there were quite a lot of popular "football" sports being played throughout the world and, of course, England. Many of these sports had similar rules and eventually, on October 26, 1863, a group of teams in England decided to get together and create a standard set of rules which would be used at all of their matches. They formed the rules for "Association Football," with the "Association" distinguishing it from the many other types of football sports in existence in England, such as "Rugby Football."

British school boys of the day liked to nickname everything, which is still somewhat common. They also liked to add the ending "er" to these nicknames. Thus, Rugby was at that time popularly called "Rugger." Association Football was then much better known as "Assoccer," which quickly just became "Soccer" and sometimes "Soccer Football."

The inventor of the nickname is said to be Charles Wredford-Brown, who was an Oxford student around the time of Association Football's inception, though the story behind this is most likely legend. The legend goes that in 1863, shortly after the creation of Association Football, some of Wredford-Brown's friends asked him if he'd come play a game of "Rugger," to which he replied he preferred "Soccer." Whether that story's true or not, around this time the name did indeed catch on amongst the masses.

In the beginning, the newly standardized Rugby and Soccer were football sports for "gentlemen," primarily being played by the upper echelons of society. However, these two forms of football gradually spread to the masses, particularly Soccer as Rugby didn't really catch on too well with the lower classes.

As Soccer became the dominant football sport, this resulted in the name switching from "Soccer" and "Association Football," to just "Football"; with the first documented case of the sport being called by the singular term "Football" coming in 1881.

From here, the game gradually spread throughout the world under the name "Football." The problem was, though, that a lot of other countries already had popular sports of their own that they called "Football," such as the United States, Canada, Ireland, Australia, New Zealand, and South Africa, to name a few. In these countries, the name "Soccer" was and, in some still is, preferred for this reason.

Essentially, the most popular football sport in a given region, tends to be called by the generic "football," with others given a more distinguishing name.

BONUS FACT

Most of the earliest forms of Football were named thus, not because you kicked a ball with your foot, but because they were played on foot, to distinguish them from sports played on horseback. Thus, games played on foot were called "XYZ Football," whether they had anything to do with kicking a ball or not. Indeed, many of the earliest forms of football involved carrying balls in an attempt to get across goal lines passed some opposing team or individual players.

WHY CERTAIN AMERICAN FOOTBALL GAMES ARE CALLED "BOWLS"

In 1901, the Roses Association sponsored a college Tournament East-West football game between Michigan and Stanford. In this game, Stanford quit in the third quarter, being down 49-0. For the next 15 years, this annual event stopped featuring football, and rather featured other events such as chariot racing. However, in 1916 the Roses Association decided to sponsor a football tournament once again, this time between WSU (then called "The State College of Washington") and Brown. This game was held at Tournament Park in Pasadena, as were subsequent annual matches. Fast-forward five years and they had need of a stadium to play the game at since attendance for this tournament had swelled massively.

Myron Hunt was commissioned to design a stadium for this purpose, which was completed two years later and named Rose Bowl. Like many other college football stadiums since, Rose Bowl was modeled after the design of Yale's stadium, Yale Bowl, which got its name from the fact that it resembled a bowl, much like Rose Bowl. This tournament sponsored by the Roses Association was then named the "Rose Bowl," after the stadium.

Gradually other cities and universities with football teams saw the money making opportunities and promotional value of these tournament games and began creating their own "bowl" games, even though many of these games were not played in bowl shaped stadiums.

The NFL eventually borrowed this terminology when they created the Pro Bowl in 1951. In 1970, the AFL and NFL merged and they created a championship game called the "AFL-NFL World Championship Game". This game was called such for two years while the final details of the merger were being worked out. Upon the third "AFL-NFL World Championship Game" the merger was complete and this championship game was re-branded the "Super Bowl," after the college naming convention. This third match-up, being called "Super Bowl III," also set the tradition of using Roman numerals for the Super Bowl, rather than the year of the game.

WHY CHOCOLATE IS BAD FOR DOGS

Chocolate contains an alkaloid called "theobromine." Theobromine is in the same family as caffeine and is a type of stimulant (they both are mythylxanines). Theobromine stimulates the central nervous system and cardiovascular system, and it causes slightly increased blood pressure.

Dogs and certain other animals, such as horses and cats, cannot metabolize theobromine as quickly as humans can; this causes the above effects to be much more severe than is the case with humans. The specific notable side effects of toxic levels of theobromine in dogs includes: diarrhea; vomiting; increased urination; muscle twitching; excessive panting; hyperactive behavior; whining; dehydration; digestive problems; seizures; and rapid heart rate. Some of these symptoms, like the rapid heart rate, can ultimately be fatal to the dog.

So how much chocolate is too much for a dog? That depends on the size and age of the dog, as well as what type of chocolate is consumed. The larger the dog, the more theobromine they can handle without dying and older dogs tend to have more problems with the side effects.

As far as the chocolate itself, cocoa powder contains about sixteen times as much theobromine per ounce over milk chocolate, with most popular forms of chocolate falling somewhere between those two, excepting white chocolate, which contains insignificant amounts of theobromine per ounce, making it extremely unlikely that a dog could, or ever would, consume enough to be harmful.

So, the general rules for the amount of chocolate that will be toxic for a dog:

- Milk chocolate: one ounce per pound of body weight (so, without intervention, a 16-pound dog (7.2 kilogram) would likely die from eating one pound of milk chocolate)
- Dark chocolate: 1/3 of an ounce per pound of body weight (around 5 ounces of dark chocolate for that same 16-pound dog)
- Baker's chocolate: 1/9 of an ounce per pound of body weight (around 1.8 ounces of baker's chocolate for a

16-pound dog)
- Cocoa powder: 1/16 of an ounce per pound of dog (around 1 ounce of cocoa powder to kill a 16-pound dog)

On the other extreme end, it would take about 200 pounds of white chocolate consumed within a 17-hour period to reach toxic levels of theobromine for a 16-pound dog. The low quantity of theobromine here is because white chocolate is made from cocoa butter, sugar, and milk, not cocoa solids.

BONUS FACT

Once the theobromine is in the dog's bloodstream, the half-life is around 17.5 hours, so 24 hours or so after the dog has consumed the chocolate, if it is still alive, it's probably going to make it.

WHY HOMOSEXUAL PEOPLE ARE CALLED "GAY"

The word "gay" seems to have its origins around the twelfth century in England, derived from the Old French word "gai," which in turn was probably derived from a Germanic word, though that isn't known for certain. The word's original meaning meant something to the effect of "joyful," "carefree," "full of mirth," or "bright and showy."

However, around the early parts of the seventeenth century, the word began to be associated with immorality. By the mid-seventeenth century, according to the *Oxford English Dictionary*, the meaning of the word had changed to mean, "addicted to pleasures and dissipations. Often euphemistically: Of loose and immoral life." This is an extension of one of the original meanings of "carefree," meaning more or less "uninhibited."

Fast-forward to the nineteenth century and the word "gay" had evolved to refer to a woman who was a prostitute and, funny enough, a gay man was someone who slept with a lot of women, often prostitutes. Also at this time, the phrase "gay it" meant to have sex.

With these new definitions, the original meanings of "carefree," "joyful," and "bright and showy" were still around; so the word was not exclusively used to refer to prostitutes or a promiscuous man. Those were just accepted definitions, along with the other meanings of the word.

Around the 1920s and 1930s, however, the word started to have a new meaning. In terms of the sexual meaning of the word, a "gay man" no longer just meant a man who had sex with a lot of women, but now started to refer to men who had sex with other men. There was also another phrase "gey cat" at this time which meant "homosexual boy."

By 1955, "gay" had popularly acquired the newly added definition of "homosexual male." Gay men themselves seem to have been behind the driving thrust for this new definition as they felt (and most still do) that "homosexual" was much too clinical sounding and thus is often thought of as slightly offensive among gay people due to sounding like a disorder.

As such, it was common amongst themselves to refer to one another as "gay" decades before this was a popularly known definition (reportedly homosexual men were calling one another "gay" as early as the 1920s). At this time, homosexual women were still referred to as "lesbians," not gay. Although, women could still be called "gay" if they were prostitutes as that meaning had not yet wholly disappeared.

Since then, "gay," meaning "homosexual male," has steadily driven out all the other definitions that have floated about through time, and it has gradually begun supplementing the word "lesbian" as referring to women who are homosexual.

BONUS FACT

Bringing Up Baby in 1938 is thought to be the first film to use the word "gay" to mean "homosexual." In one scene, Cary Grant had to wear a lady's feathery robe. When another character asks why he is wearing that, he responds with an ad-libbed line, "Because I just went gay." At the time, mainstream audiences didn't get the reference so the line was popularly thought to have meant something to the effect of, "I just decided to be carefree."

WHY LEAVES CHANGE COLOR IN THE AUTUMN

The primary thing that triggers the changing of colors in leaves is the length of day. However, moisture and temperature play a role as well. For instance, an extreme drought in the summer can delay, somewhat, the changing of the colors in autumn. Why this is the case is not wholly understood, but it is possibly from the tree not being able to make as much food to store up for the winter, in the case of the drought, so it might be trying to push the envelope a little in terms of making food for a couple more weeks before needing to shed the leaves.

Temperature also plays a part in the ultimate vividness of the color. However, as far as the timing of the change goes, it seems to play only a small role given that trees of the same species at very high elevations, where it is colder, will have their leaves change color at nearly the same time as those of the same species at lower elevations on the same latitude line.

Primarily though, as the length of day shortens, at a certain point that varies by species, some mechanism in the tree will trigger it to begin the process of closing up the veins to the leaves and eventually shedding them, lest they freeze while the veins are still open which can potentially harm the tree.

There are three main things that give leaves their color. Those are: chlorophyll (green), which is necessary for photosynthesis; carotenoids, such as carotene and xanthophylls, which produce the orange and yellow colors, but whose roles are not entirely understood; and anthocyanins, which give us the shades of red and purple.

In the former two cases of chlorophyll and carotenoids, they are both present in the leaves during the summer, but the chlorophyll more or less drowns out the carotenoids, so you see a mostly green leaf, rather than orange or yellow. The anthocyanins, on the other hand, are primarily produced as a result of glucose that is trapped in the leaves when the veins are closed off. These sugars then break down as a result of sunlight and produce the red and purple pigments.

During the summer, the plant is continually producing

chlorophyll to aid in the production of glucose, which the tree uses for food. Once the day length decreases sufficiently, the tree gradually starts to decrease the production of chlorophyll and the veins to the leaves slowly close off. When this happens, what you have left is the carotenoids and, depending on the species and environmental factors, possibly the produced anthocyanins.

BONUS FACT

The most vivid colors on tree leaves can typically be observed after a succession of very warm sunny days in autumn, which in turn give way to cold, but not freezing, nights. This is a result of the fact that a lot of sugars will be produced in the daytime in these leaves, assuming there is still moisture present, but the veins in the leaves will be closed off, or nearly closed off, so the sugars remain in the leaves. This spurs production of the anthocyanin pigments. If there are also carotenoids present, you'll see from this some vivid leaves which may contain some mix of yellow/orange/red/purple colors.

WHY BREATHING HELIUM CHANGES THE SOUND OF YOUR VOICE

First, it is necessary to explain a little about how you actually generate sound via your voice box. The air in your lungs gets pushed up by the relaxation of your diaphragm. It then goes through your trachea and out a small orifice that has two folds of skin (vocal cords) on either side of it, in the shape of a V. This is called your larynx or voice box. As the muscles that attach to your voice box tense and relax, they create a vibration of the cords. As these cords vibrate, they release pulses of air. The tension in these muscles creates the differences in frequency. The higher the tension, the higher the frequency and therefore the higher the pitch. This frequency is measured in hertz (how many times per second this repeats). For example, nearly all human speech sounds usually range from approximately 200 hertz to 8,000 hertz. Meaning the sound waves vibrate at approximately 200 to 8,000 times per second.

Once out of the voice box, the air travels into the area of your mouth that can be informally known as your vocal tract. As you manipulate your tongue, jaw and lips, you can change the resonant frequencies created by your vocal cords, allowing you to make the many different sounds of speech.

Together, the sound we hear created by air flowing at different frequencies and resonances creates our voices. One other factor affecting pitch is the thickness of one's vocal cords. The thicker the folds of skin are, the deeper the voice. This is due to the amount of mass your chords have that the air has to manipulate. As you would expect, men tend to have much thicker folds of skin then women.

So now let's talk about the air that comes out of your lungs. The number of molecules in a fixed volume of gas, like the volume of air in your lungs, does not change with the type of gas (assuming the pressures are reasonably low). As long as the temperature and the pressure are the same, it does not matter whether it is helium or air; the number of molecules is the same. The mass of those molecules is then measured by atomic weight. Atomic weight is a dimensionless physical quantity (which is why it works so well for a gas that does not necessarily have a given dimension). It is the ratio of the average mass of atoms of an element compared to one-twelfth of the mass of an atom of carbon-12. All that basically means is the higher the number, the heavier the gas.

Helium has an atomic weight of 4.002602. Air which is approximately 80% Nitrogen, has differing characteristics depending on the environment. (for instance if you live in Los Angeles its about 99.99% car exhaust...) Because of this, air's actual atomic weight is impossible to precisely define. However, it is generally about seven times heavier than helium.

So why the perceived difference in your voice with helium? The answer lies in how sound waves travel through a given gas. The more dense, or heavier, the gas, the slower the sound wave will travel. Helium is much lighter than air. The speed of a sound wave through helium will then be much higher. So by inhaling helium and using it as the source of the perceived sound, you are simply increasing the speed or frequency of your voice. You are not changing the pitch, since your vocal chords are vibrating at the same speed as when you are using air. You are also not changing the configuration of your vocal tract. So while the base frequency of the chords remains the same, the frequency of the sound heard by others is increased due to the wave traveling through helium much faster than through air.

BONUS FACT

Inhaling a gas that is heavier than air, such as xenon, will have the opposite effect of helium and make your voice sound deeper. This, however, is extremely dangerous as gases heavier than air tend to settle at the bottom of your lungs, thereby not allowing air to enter those spaces, and potentially suffocating you.

WHY CERTAIN TYPES OF TRAPS ARE CALLED "BOOBY TRAPS"

It turns out this has nothing to do with the mammaries of the fairer sex, but rather has its origins in the Spanish word "bobo," meaning "stupid," "fool," or "naïve." This Spanish word in turn comes from the Latin "balbus" meaning "stammering", which to the Romans was thought to be a sign of stupidity.

So, essentially, a "booby trap" is a trap that "boobies," or idiots, are the victims of. Around the same time this first popped up, we also had expressions like "booby prize," meaning a prize given to a fool. These prizes were usually something completely valueless and often given to the loser of some competition, with the first instance of this appearing in the late nineteenth century.

In the early days, "booby traps" were just simple pranks. As you might expect, the first known instances of this applied to school boys pulling pranks on one another, with the victim then being considered a booby or fool.

For instance, one of the earliest known instances of "booby trap" appeared in the 1868 *Chambers Journal* where it stated: "A 'booby-trap' - it consisted ... of books, boots, etc., balanced on the top of a door, which was left ajar, so that the first incomer got a solid shower-bath."

Fast-forward about a half a century and booby traps got a lot more deadly with the WWI usage of calling deadly explosive traps "booby traps."

BONUS FACT

The word "booby," in English, first popped up in the sense of "fool" or "dummy" around the late sixteenth century and was within decades applied to birds of the Sula genus. These birds have very large feet that make them look clumsy and foolish when they walk or run, instead of fly. In addition, they would often land on ships and were exceptionally easy to catch, making them popular fair for sailors, who began calling these birds "boobies" for their perceived stupidity.

WHY VOICES SQUEAK DURING PUBERTY

In case you skipped the "Why Breathing Helium Changes the Sound of Your Voice", I'll briefly sum up how the human vocal system works here. Once you activate your vocal system, the air in your lungs gets pushed up by the relaxation of your diaphragm. It then goes through your trachea and out a small orifice that has two folds of skin (vocal cords) on either side of it, in the shape of a V; this is called your larynx, or voice box. As the muscles that attach to your voice box tense to varying degrees, they create a vibration of the cords. As these cords vibrate, they release pulses of air. The tension in these muscles creates the differences in frequency, the higher the tension, the higher the frequency and, therefore, the higher the pitch.

When we are kids, our larynx is relatively small and our vocal cords are relatively thin. Think of guitar strings, the smaller and thinner the string, the higher the pitch. As boys go through puberty, the increasing amounts of testosterone leads to a lengthening of the cartilage of the larynx and a thickening of the vocal folds. This lengthening and thickening deepens the tone in their voices, similar to the effect of lengthening and thickening a guitar string. Along with the "guitar strings" of the voice box getting bigger, there are also other features affecting the sound of one's voice that are changing. For instance, things like the nose, back of the throat (hypopharnyx), sinuses and facial bones getting bigger will affect the ultimate sound of the voice. These bigger features create more space in your facial area, giving your vocal sounds more room to resonate.

The changes to the voice box generally take place gradually over a period of time. Sometimes, however, when there is a dramatic period of change, the body has not "grown into" its newly sized cords and vocal mechanism and has trouble adjusting, in terms of being able to make steady sounds. So the sudden and differing growth rates of everything involved in making sounds causes the brain to sometimes have a hard time controlling the voice mechanism to maintain a steady vibrating resonance. As a result of this, poor little Billy must endure his voice cracking from time to time while his brain adjusts to the quick changes his body is going through.

WHY DOUGHNUTS HAVE HOLES

Because bakers make them that way… In truth, nobody knows with 100% certainty why people started putting holes in the fried cakes. There are some outlandish tales from a sailor, Captain Hanson Gregory, who claimed to have invented the holed doughnut in 1847 at the age of 16. There is even a plaque in Rockport, Maine near Clam Cove that states, "In commemoration. This is the birthplace of Captain Hanson Gregory, who first invented the hole in the doughnut in 1847. Erected by his friends, Nov. 2, 1947."

There are a variety of versions of this tale, but the version Gregory put forth in the Washington Post (Mar. 26, 1916) was as follows:

"Now in them days we used to cut the doughnuts into diamond shapes, and also into long strips, bent in half, and then twisted. I don't think we called them doughnuts then—they was just 'fried cakes' and 'twisters.'

"Well, sir, they used to fry all right around the edges, but when you had the edges done the insides was all raw dough. And the twisters used to sop up all the grease just where they bent, and they were tough on the digestion.

"Well, I says to myself, 'Why wouldn't a space inside solve the difficulty?' I thought at first I'd take one of the strips and roll it around, then I got an inspiration, a great inspiration.

"I took the cover off the ship's tin pepper box, and—I cut into the middle of that doughnut the first hole ever seen by mortal eyes!

"…Well, sir, them doughnuts was the finest I ever tasted. No more indigestion—no more greasy sinkers—but just well-done, fried-through doughnuts."

He then claims to have taught this to a variety of people and thanks to being a sailor, the holed doughnut idea spread throughout the world.

Color me skeptical… Besides the fact that these types of historical anecdotes are almost never wholly accurate or even true at all, Gregory seems to have changed the details of the tale significantly as he aged. Whether this is true or not, most bakers do think that the reason doughnuts have holes is the reason Captain Gregory stated: to get rid of the slightly doughy center.

However, given the timing of when holed doughnuts first popped up, and given that people have been frying up dough and making doughnut-like cakes for centuries and no one thought there was much need to remove the center, excepting some who would put fruit and the like there instead, an alternative theory has been proposed, which to me seems much more plausible. It is simply that holes in the middle of doughnuts made a convenient way to display the cakes for sale.

Around the same time doughnuts with holes popped up (first in New York City), bagels were also becoming very popular in New York and were commonly put on display stacked on wooden dowels. It may simply be that bakers in New York first got the bright idea to put holes in the dough before frying when one or more of them thought to display the doughnuts in the same way as bagels, on dowels, which no doubt saved display space. With this theory, producing a more evenly fried product may or may not have come into play.

WHY YOU USED TO HAVE TO USE #2 PENCILS ON SCANTRONS

Now, you might be saying, "Used to? Don't you still have to?" It turns out, despite what pretty much all teachers will tell you, not really. Modern Scantron systems are quite high-tech, using image sensors and sophisticated image processing algorithms. These algorithms can even pick out which oval has the strongest mark. So if your test is being processed by one of these newer Scantron systems, you could fill out every bubble on the Scantron and it would simply pick the darkest shaded bubble in each row and assign that as your answer.

As such, you can use pens, pencils, and even printer toner or ink, if you want to run your Scantron through a printer to mark all your answers. Pencils are obviously still preferred over pens, giving you the ability to erase your answer. Also, generally speaking, you still want to use some form of grey to black colored marking device to ensure your Scantron form is read perfectly. Although, anecdotal evidence has shown that even using shades of different colored ink or colored pencils will also work. Though, at that point, the system isn't necessarily going to read your form perfectly. Further, if you pick a shade that is the exact color of the lines on the form, it might just ignore your markings.

On the flip-side, the early models of Scantron machines were significantly less sophisticated. They read pencil marks by shining light through the paper and Lucite light guides. The light was then received through phototubes. With this antiquated system, for an answer to be read, the light must be completely blocked out by the pencil marking to register correctly.

Graphite works well for this purpose because graphite molecules, which form tiny sheets of carbon, reflect much of the light that hits them and absorb most all the rest. It turns out, black ink isn't opaque enough for these old Scantron systems. Further, lighter shades of graphite, such as in #3 and #4 pencils, weren't sufficiently opaque enough for these old systems to perform without error, as is generally required. #1 pencils would have worked fine, as they are darker than #2 pencils. But, unfortunately, they also smudge easier when erased or accidentally rubbed with your hand as you mark the Scantron form, increasing the possibility of a "false positive" when the Scantron was reading your form. So #2 pencils were just the right mix of darkness and hardness of the graphite/clay core to block the light effectively, while also not smudging too much.

One of the ways you can tell instantly whether whoever is processing your Scantron is using a modern system or not is if the Scantron is double-sided. If so, it cannot be using an antiquated model, as the marks on the other side would interfere with the older system's ability to correctly read the scantron form. Modern systems have no such problem.

WHY PENCIL LEAD IS CALLED "LEAD"

In the sixteenth century, a large deposit of pure, solid graphite was discovered in Borrowdale, England. This was the first time in recorded history that high quality, solid graphite had been found. When metallurgists first encountered this substance, they thought it was some sort of black lead, rather than a form of carbon. Thus, they called it "plumbago", which is derived from "plumbum," which is Latin for "lead."

It didn't take people long to realize that solid sticks of high quality graphite were good for marking things. At that point, the graphite from the mines of Borrowdale became extremely valuable. So much so that guards were eventually posted at the entrance to the mine and laws were passed to stop people from stealing the solid graphite. In addition, once a sufficient stock of the graphite was mined, the mine itself would be flooded until more graphite was needed.

Unfortunately, sticks of pure graphite are fairly brittle, so people started embedding it in various things such as hollowed out pieces of wood and also simply wrapped tightly in sheep skin. Thus, the pencil was officially born with a core of solid graphite, which was known then as "black lead." The tradition of calling sticks of graphite "lead" has endured to this day.

BONUS FACT

English speakers aren't the only ones who still follow this misnomer. The German word for "pencil" is actually "bleistift," which literally means "lead stick."

WHY IODINE IS ADDED TO SALT

Iodine first began being added to salt commercially in the United States in 1924 by the Morton Salt Company at the request of the government. This was done as a response to the fact that there were certain regions in the U.S., such as around the Great Lakes and in the Pacific Northwest, where people weren't getting enough iodine in their diets due to it not being prevalent in the soil in those regions. Among other problems, this caused many people to develop goiters (swelling of the thyroid gland).

About 90% of people who develop a goiter do so because of a lack of iodine in their diets, so the simple solution was to add iodine to something pretty much everyone consumes fairly regularly, namely salt. This practice was not thought up by the U.S. but was copied from the Swiss who were adding iodine to salt at this time for the same reason. This resulted in researchers at the University of Michigan testing this practice out with good results and subsequently the Morton Salt Company adopted the practice on a national level.

This didn't cost Morton and the other salt companies that followed suit much money, only a few cents per person per year in iodine, but it drastically cut down the number of people who developed goiters in the United States and beyond as the practice gradually became adopted throughout much of the developed world.

Today, because most food in developed countries like the United States often isn't grown locally, coming from all over the country and world, continuing to add iodine to salt isn't strictly necessary. People in regions where the soil is lacking in iodine will likely consume plenty of food from regions where it is not, thus getting the iodine their bodies need, particularly because our thyroids don't need much to function properly.

For reference, the U.S. Food and Drug Administration recommends that you consume about 150 micrograms of iodine per day and, on average, men in the United States get about double that amount per day and women each consume about 210 micrograms of iodine per day. Your thyroid itself only needs about 70 micrograms per day to function properly.

Even though most people get plenty of Iodine in their diets, because Iodine is so critical to our bodies functioning properly and the Tolerable Upper Intake Level is so high (about 1,100 micrograms per day, and you won't take a fatal dose unless you ingest about 2 million micrograms, or 2 grams), adding it to salt is still recommended by many government health agencies the world over to stave off certain health problems.

For instance, Iodine is a critical element used by your thyroid in being able to synthesize certain gland secretions which, among other things, influences your heart, metabolism, nerve responses, etc. Further, a lack of iodine during pregnancy and in the baby's diet after being born can cause a myriad of significant health and developmental problems. Iodine deficiency has also been linked to increased difficulty with information processing, diminished fine motor skills, extreme fatigue, depression, weight gain, and low basal body temperatures, among other things.

WHY THE MOON LOOKS BIGGER ON THE HORIZON THAN WHEN IT IS HIGHER IN THE SKY

This is a question that has been debated for several thousand years. One popular myth, dating all the way back to Aristotle in the fourth century BC and which still endures somewhat today, is that it is simply a case of magnification caused by the Earth's atmosphere. While a "magnification" effect is taking place, it actually is going the other way and is more of a compression. Atmospheric refraction causes the Moon to appear slightly smaller in the vertical axis when it is near the horizon vs. when it is high in the sky. This refraction, combined with the fact that the Moon is about 4,000 miles farther away when it is on the horizon, causes it to appear 1.5% smaller, if you were to measure very precisely its apparent size on the horizon vs. higher in the sky.

So if it's not magnification from the Earth's atmosphere, what is going on here? In short, the Moon appearing bigger near the horizon is nothing more than an optical illusion. It's really as simple as that. You can verify this fact by taking a pair of calipers, or even just a ruler, and measure the diameter of the Moon on the horizon; later that night, when it is higher in the sky, measure it again. (Be sure and hold the measuring device at the same distance away from your eyes each time to get accurate results.) If you do it precisely enough, you'll find that it actually will measure about the same size both times, despite appearing nearly twice as big to your brain when it is on the horizon.

Exactly what is going on in our brains to cause this optical illusion is still somewhat up for debate, but it seems to center around size consistency, where our brains are trying to grapple with the size of an object vs. how far away it thinks it is. For instance, when you see people very far away from you and their heads look incredibly tiny, your brain doesn't think for an instant that the people and their heads are actually tiny. Your brain adjusts your perception based on what else is in your vision to gather that third dimension of depth.

Something of this same effect is thought to be happening with the Moon, only this time your brain is getting tricked into thinking that the Moon is farther away when it is on the horizon, making it appear bigger to you. This is known as a Ponzo Illusion, named after Italian psychologist Mario Ponzo.

Mario Ponzo first demonstrated the "Ponzo Illusion" in 1913. In this experiment, Ponzo drew two converging vertical lines on a piece of paper. He then drew two horizontal lines crossing these lines, one at the top, and one at the bottom. These two horizontal lines are the same length, but it appears that the one at the top is much longer because it appears farther away. This is due to our brains interpreting the two converging lines as parallel lines that only appear to be converging because they are getting farther away. Thus, if both horizontal lines are making the same length "imprint" on our eyes, but one is farther away, then the one that is farther away must be much larger, so our brains perceive it as larger than it actually is.

So, in the end, it's a matter of our brain's getting tricked in terms of the distance from the Moon to us when it's on the horizon vs. high in the sky. When it's on the horizon, the brain has reference points to compare and judge the distance, and similarly adjust the apparent size based on that perceived distance. When it is high in the sky, there is nothing useful to compare it to, so the apparent size changes based on how far away our brain thinks it is at that point, namely, thinking that it is closer to us high in the sky and farther away on the horizon.

WHY PEPPERS TASTE HOT

The heat sensation is caused by capsaicin, which is a colorless, odorless, oily chemical found in peppers. Capsaicin binds with certain sensory neurons which then more or less trick your body into thinking that it is being burned or at least experiencing excessive amounts of heat in the area that the capsaicin comes in contact with, even though no actual physical burning is occurring.

Specifically, what is going on is that the capsaicin is binding to the vanilloid receptor (VR1), which is a member of the superfamily TRP ion channel and thus is referred to as TRPV1; by binding to the VR1 receptor, the capsaicin molecule will produce the same sensation that normal heat will produce when activating the TRP receptors. Thus, your mouth feels really hot, even though it's not.

In extreme cases where exposure to capsaicin is high, such as in pure capsaicin extract, the sensation can be so "hot" that the body will be tricked into inflaming itself; so it would appear as if you are actually burned, even though the capsaicin doesn't actually burn you at all, just tricks your brain into thinking it's being burned.

Capsaicin is not just a substance that makes your food extra tasty, it is also used in "pepper spray", hence the name. Anytime relatively undiluted capsaicin comes in contact with your skin, particularly your eyes or breathed into your lungs, it will cause you to feel like you are being burned, even though you aren't. So it makes a very effective deterrent without actually causing any real damage to the person being sprayed; or rather I should say causes no real damage if it's not too strong a level of capsaicin.

Most of the capsaicin in peppers tends to be centered around the seeds themselves. This is a defense mechanism that the plants use to keep fungus, animals, and bugs that would destroy the seeds from wanting to eat the peppers.

One of the animals that capsaicin has no effect on is birds. Birds also can't really chew the seeds. Thus, when the birds eat the fruit and then pass the seeds through their digestive tracts, they deposit them all over the place. Humans are about the only "animals" that eat peppers that actually do tend to destroy the seeds through mashing them with our teeth. Almost all other animals/fungi/bugs that would destroy the seeds are repelled by the capsaicin

WHY MINT TASTES COLD

At a high level, what is going on here is that a chemical in mint, menthol, tricks the brain into thinking that the area the menthol is applied to is cold.

More specifically, menthol binds with cold-sensitive receptors; these receptors contain ion channels, with the most pertinent one in this case being TRPM8. The menthol makes these much more sensitive than normal, which makes your brain think you are feeling a cold sensation, when in fact, everything is more or less the same temperature as before.

This extra sensitivity is why when you eat peppermint, which has a relatively high level of menthol, and then you breathe in deeply through your mouth, your mouth feels extra cold. Your cold receptors are reacting much more easily than they normally would to the air, which is cooler than the inside of your mouth.

BONUS FACT

Mint leaves or mint oil containing high levels of menthol will also help repel mosquitoes and can even do more than just repel them; it has been shown that mint oil can actually kill the mosquitoes.

WHY THE ADAM'S APPLE IS CALLED THE ADAM'S APPLE

The origin of this term goes all the way back to the Biblical event where Eve gave Adam a forbidden fruit, which is commonly misrepresented as an apple. The term basically comes from the legend that when Adam ate of the "apple," the piece of fruit got stuck in his throat and made a lump.

Now, of course, according to the Bible story, it wasn't an apple Adam and Eve ate of, it was a fruit from the Tree of the Knowledge of Good and Evil, of which there was apparently only one. Besides the obvious fact that I don't know anyone who's felt particularly more knowledgeable in the ways of good and evil when they ate an apple, an apple tree is not self-pollinating; so you'd need more than one to have it produce more of itself, which pretty firmly kills the whole "apple tree" theory.

To make the origins of the term even more ridiculous, even if it was an apple and it got stuck in his throat, his male children wouldn't somehow miraculously also have apples stuck in their throats. This is about as absurd as the age-old "Well if Adam had a rib taken out to make Eve, why aren't men missing a rib?" Or the equally ludicrous corresponding claim by many that men are somehow missing a rib. Both sides of the argument seem to have suspended all logic while arguing over this triviality. The really funny part here is the "rib" translation was actually a *mistranslation*, more on that in a bit.

At this point you might be wondering, "Why do most people say that Bible says Adam and Eve ate an apple to get them tossed out of the Garden of Eden?" Why not an orange or a peach, or why not just call it like it is stated in the Bible story? Well, Aquila Ponticus, who was a second century translator translating the Old Testament from Hebrew to Greek, took the liberty of translating it as an apple tree, even though the original text doesn't say that. It's likely that he chose this because he was translating it into Greek for Greeks, and in Greek mythology apples were seen as symbols of desire and destruction.

The "Adam's Apple" itself is really just a result of an enlarged larynx, with the part sticking out being the thyroid cartilage, which is one of the nine cartilages that make up the laryngeal skeleton. In most men and some women, this becomes big enough to be visible in the neck.

The larynx's primary purpose is as a voice box. It also has an alternative purpose in aiding in the process of closing off the airways in your throat when you swallow. This is why it generally seems to disappear when you swallow, as it is being pulled upward to aid in this process. Around puberty, both men and women's voice boxes get bigger, along with a thickening of the vocal folds. This, in turn, makes voices deeper, with men's larynges growing more than women's and thus typically making for a deeper voice and more prominent bump.

Now back to the "rib" misconception. The original Hebrew word used here "צלע" (tsela) comes from the root word of "צלע" (tsala), which means "curve." So, in the Biblical story, it in essence says God took something from Adam's "side" or "curve" to make Eve. It should be noted here that though "tsela" is used plenty of other places in the Bible, it never refers to a rib in those instances. Indeed, the one place a rib is mentioned, it is using a completely different Hebrew word. It is also important to note that Hebrew priests from about 2,000 years ago went with the "side" meaning and not "rib," which is something that's once again coming back into common practice.

WHY ZIPPERS HAVE "YKK" ON THEM

The YKK stands for Yoshida Kogyo Kabushikikaisha. In 1934, Tadao Yoshida founded Yoshida Kogyo Kabushikikaisha (translated, this means Yoshida Industries Limited). This company is now the world's foremost zipper manufacturer, making about 90% of all zippers in over 206 facilities in 52 countries. In fact, they not only make the zippers, they also make the machines that make the zippers.

Today, their largest factory in Georgia makes over seven million zippers per day!

Mr. Yoshida's company zipped to number one by practicing the "Cycle of Goodness," as he called it. Namely, "No one prospers unless he renders benefit to others." Using this principle, he endeavored to create the best zippers out there that would hold up over long periods of time in the end product. This, in turn, would benefit both the manufacturers who used his zippers and the end customer, while also benefiting his company with higher rates of repeat and referral sales, thus completing the "Cycle of Goodness."

So next time you're zipping up, take a moment to remember Mr. Yoshida; also, if you're going commando, careful with Captain Winky on the zip up. I can't stress that enough.

WHY THE TOILET IS CALLED A "JOHN"

The term is thought to derive from Sir John Harrington or, at the least, to have been popularized due to Harrington. (There are a few references of the toilet being called "Cousin John", as well as many references to it being called "Jake" and other such generic names, before Harrington was born; but it is generally agreed that why we now call it "John" is because of Harrington and not from the old "Cousin John").

Sir John Harrington lived in the late sixteenth and early seventeenth centuries. Harrington was one of the 102 god-children of Queen Elizabeth I, known as the "Saucy Godson," for his proclivity to write somewhat risqué poetry and other such things, which often got him banished from England only to be allowed to return again sometime later.

Along with writing several notable works, Harrington also devised one of Britain's first flushing toilets, which he called the "Ajax." This name derived from the term "Jakes," which was a slang term for what we now call a toilet.

Shortly thereafter, Harrington wrote one of his more famous and popular works titled, *A New Discourse upon a Stale Subject: The Metamorphosis of Ajax*. This, on the surface, was about his new invention, but more to the point was a political allegory on the "stercus" (excrement) that was poisoning the state.

The book got him banished from the court for a time due to its allusions to the Earl of Leicester. However, the actual flushing toilet device itself was real and was installed in his home, and around 1596 one was made for the queen. The device worked by pulling a cord that would allow water to rush in from the "water closet," which would flush away the waste.

Although Harrington wasn't by any means the first to invent a flushing toilet (there are references to flushing toilets going all the way back to around 2600 BC), his invention was an innovation in Britain at the time and it was commonly thought there that he was the inventor of the flushing toilet, which is why even today it is sometimes called a "John."

WHY "TAKE ME OUT TO THE BALL GAME" IS SUNG DURING THE SEVENTH INNING STRETCH OF MAJOR LEAGUE BASEBALL GAMES

You might be surprised to learn that this staple of Major League Baseball games is actually something of a modern practice, first starting as a regular part of the seventh inning stretch with the White Sox in the late 1970s, thanks to Hall of Fame broadcaster Harry Carabina, better known as Harry Caray.

Before this, the song had occasionally been sung by fans at various baseball games (both amateur and in the Major Leagues), but never as a regular thing nor at any designated time. The first known instance of this was at a Los Angeles high school game in 1934. It was also played before one of the games in the 1934 World Series when Pepper Martin and the St. Louis Cardinals Band played it.

Harry Caray started singing the song during the seventh inning stretch in 1971, with fans within earshot of his booth occasionally joining in.

There are conflicting accounts from those involved (including a story that changed over time from then owner, Bill Veeck) as to how this event transitioned to a White Sox tradition. In one account, after Caray refused to sing over the stadium PA system, Veeck tricked Caray by switching on Caray's microphone while he was singing. Probably, the more likely tale is another first-hand account that it was all planned out ahead of time. But that's not nearly as entertaining, so one can see why the colorful Bill Veeck might embellish the story a little.

Whatever the case, in 1976, Caray started singing the song over the stadium PA system and it became a local tradition.

When Caray switched to calling games for the Cubs in 1982, he brought this tradition with him. Thanks to the fact that WGN broadcasted the Cubs games nationally, the masses quickly learned of Harry Caray's seventh inning tradition. Shortly thereafter, variations on this tradition were adopted at other stadiums, with the song in question varying from team to team. In the end, all teams went ahead and went with *Take Me Out to the Ballgame*.

Despite the fact that singing *Take Me Out to the Ballgame* during the seventh inning stretch is a modern practice, the song itself, about a girl named Katie Case who wants her boyfriend to take her to a baseball game, has been around since 1908 when it was written by famed song writer Jack Norworth (who wrote over 2,500 songs in his lifetime, including a couple dozen that sold more than a million copies each). The music was composed by Albert Von Tilzer.

Funny enough, both of these gentlemen had never actually been to a professional baseball game when they created the song. Norworth claimed the first Major League Baseball game he ever went to wasn't until June 27, 1940, a Dodgers / Cubs game.

So what inspired this non-baseball fan to write a baseball song? While riding a train to Manhattan, Norworth said he saw a sign that said "Baseball Today – Polo Grounds" and simply decided to write a song about going to a baseball game, so he scribbled it down during his ride.

Once the song was complete, Norworth's wife, singer-actress Nora Bayes, was the first to sing it publicly. It quickly became a hit at various vaudeville acts and then beyond, becoming one of the most popular songs of 1908.

BONUS FACT

You'll often read that the seventh inning stretch tradition in baseball was thanks to President William Howard Taft in 1910. The general story goes that the extremely overweight President, after throwing out the first pitch on April 14, 1910, in a game between the Washington Senators and the Philadelphia Athletics, was uncomfortable sitting in the small stadium seating and by the seventh inning needed to stretch, so he stood up. When he did this, those in attendance noticed and everyone else stood up out of respect until Taft finally sat back down after thoroughly stretching.

Whether this actually happened or not, we do know that this was not the origin of the seventh inning stretch. The first recorded instance of the seventh inning stretch goes all the way back to the earliest days of professional baseball in 1869, where Harry Wright, who played for the Cincinnati Red Stockings at the time, wrote in a letter, "The spectators all arise between halves of the seventh inning, extend their legs and arms, and sometimes walk about. In so doing, they enjoy the relief afforded by relaxation from a long posture upon hard benches."

There are also other documented instances of the practice of the seventh inning stretch in both professional and amateur games before Taft. So while it's true that Taft did indeed throw out the first pitch of the game in question, and given the seventh inning stretch was already around, I'm even willing to buy that he stood up and stretched at the appointed time. But, it would seem the reason the masses stood too was simply because this was already an established practice. That being said, it wasn't specifically called the "seventh-inning stretch" until the 1920s.

WHY MILK IS WHITE

Milk consists of about 87% water and 13% solids, such as fat and various proteins. Chief among these proteins is something called casein, four types of which make up about 80% of the proteins in milk. The casein protein molecules are typically suspended somewhat uniformly throughout the milk and are spherical, about a micrometer across. The reason they are somewhat uniformly suspended in the liquid is because kappa-casein molecules have a negative electrical charge, so they repel each other.

White objects in nature appear such when there is some level of light diffusion going on and no part of the visible spectrum gets reflected off the object any more than any other part of that area of the light spectrum. So as you might guess, these casein proteins and some of the fats in the milk scatter and deflect light somewhat uniformly throughout the visual spectrum. This results in milk being fairly opaque and appearing white to our eyes. Without the fats though, casein itself tends to scatter the blue wavelength slightly more than red. So with something such as fat free skimmed milk, you'll sometimes see a very slight blue-ish tinge to the otherwise white milk because of this.

Milk also contains riboflavin, which can give the milk a slightly green-ish tinge, if the concentration is large enough, such as can also be seen sometimes in certain types of skimmed milk or whey products (the riboflavin is in the whey portion of the milk).

Another hue you'll occasionally see in milk is a slight yellow color. When you see this, it is due to small amounts of carotene that are present in the milk. You will see this particularly in milk from Guernsey and Jersey cattle.

WHY LOBSTERS TURN RED WHEN COOKED

Typically, the exoskeleton of most crustaceans has a blue-green to grayish color, and sometimes they appear a brown or olive green, with just a hint of red (with a few exceptions like the blue and yellow lobsters and crabs). The exoskeletons of such creatures are made up of several pigments, one of which is a carotenoid called astaxanthin, that provide its reddish coloring (astaxanthin is the same carotene that gives salmon its color).

At normal temperatures and when alive (in other words, when we're not dumping them in boiling water or grilling the poor guys), the astaxanthin pigments are hidden because they are covered with other protein chains that give their shells the bluish-gray or brownish-green color we see.

Exposure to heat destroys this protein coating, while the carotenoid pigment, astaxanthin still remains stable. So when you cook a crab or lobster or its other tasty crustacean friends, the heat breaks down all the pigments except for astaxanthin, thus, causing the bright red color we see in cooked lobsters, crabs, and crayfish or the reddish-orange color of cooked shrimp.

Now you might be wondering, "What about the very rare, 1 in 2 million blue lobster? Does it turn red when cooked?" YES! Even the more rare 1 in 30 million yellow lobster turns red. Only the albino crab and lobster do not turn red when cooked, for the obvious reason that they have no pigmentation and therefore, remain the same color even when cooked: white.

WHY YOUR STOMACH GROWLS WHEN YOU'RE HUNGRY

Generally speaking "stomach growling", or as the Greeks named it and doctors call it today "borborygmi" (which is an onomatopoeia), is the noise created during rhythmic muscle contractions in your stomach and intestines.

Your digestive system is basically one big long tube that goes from your mouth to your butt, with a lot of interesting biological machinery in-between. The body gets food through this long tube via waves of muscle contractions, called "peristalsis," that run a few inches at a time down your digestive tract. These waves of muscle contractions also serve to mix and churn foods, liquids, and digestive juices together. The resulting cocktail is called "chime."

These waves of contractions are really not too dissimilar to how your heart-beat works in that they create fluctuation of electrical potential in the smooth muscle cells, which causes the muscle to contract in a rhythmic fashion in this case, called the "Basic Electrical Rhythm" or BER.

This rhythm is about three times per minute in the stomach, and twelve times per minute in the small intestines. The sound you hear when your stomach and intestines make noise is the result of these muscular contractions mixing and moving the chyme along, as well as pushing any resultant air through your system.

So why does your stomach seem to growl more when you are hungry? When your stomach and intestines are empty, it triggers a reflexive generation of waves along your stomach and intestine muscles that trigger contractions, even though there isn't really much of anything in your stomach that needs moved along. These are meant to clear out all of your stomach contents, including the mucus, any remaining food, bacteria, etc. It's your body's way of doing a little house cleaning, making sure no food or other matter is accumulating anywhere along your stomach or intestines. It's typically this that you hear when you're hungry.

You might be asking yourself, "Well if my stomach is doing these contractions even when I'm full, moving food along, why don't I hear them all the time?" To answer that, think of the stomach as hot water bottle. When it is full and you slosh the contents around, there is little to no noise, depending on how full the bottle is. The less you have in it, the more noise the sloshing makes. This is pretty much exactly what is going on with the stomach, only the muscles lining the walls of your stomach and intestines are doing the sloshing as they push the contents of your stomach and intestines towards your derriere.

So how does one avoid stomach growling when, say, you are in a quiet classroom taking a test in school or a quiet open office space? The first trick is, when you feel a growl coming on, to take something like a pencil and quite literally push it hard into your stomach area around the point you feel the contraction starting (eraser end first of course). If you push it hard enough, it will literally compress a part of your stomach, giving it much less space to slosh or even stopping it from being able to slosh at all temporarily.

The second trick is to inhale as much as possible, filling your lungs to their max as soon as you feel a stomach growl coming on. Now hold your breath until you feel the growl sensation pass. This effectively does the same thing as the previous method, but it works from the inside with your expanded lungs pushing down on your stomach and compressing it so that it can't slosh things about as much.

WHY IT'S NEARLY IMPOSSIBLE TO TICKLE YOURSELF

It's very hard to tickle yourself because your brain anticipates things going on around you in order to help speed up response times. More technically, the cerebellum monitors body movements and can also distinguish between expected sensations and unexpected ones, generally resulting in diminishing or completely discarding expected sensations, while paying much more attention to unexpected ones.

So your brain is actively anticipating touch sensations. When it is doing this, it is also actively discarding sensations that it deems unimportant, like when you are typing and it significantly dulls the touch sensation in your fingertips so that you don't really notice it unless you consciously think about it. This same type of thing happens when you try to tickle yourself.

Researchers at University College London tested this by scanning the brains of subjects while the palms of their hands were touched by themselves and by experimenters. The brain scans revealed that when the touch was externally produced the somatosensory cortex (involved in processing touch) and anterior cingulate (involved in processing pleasure) parts of the brain reacted much more strongly than when the touch was produced by the subjects themselves. In these latter cases, the brain was using information it had on hand, such as motor movements of the finger and arms to anticipate the touch.

Results from a different study showed that the same internal anticipated response applies when subjects manipulated a robot, which then in turn manipulated another robot to touch the subject's palms. This was only true, however, when the associated touch from the second robot happened right away. When this happened, the cerebellum sends information on the sensation to expect to the somatosensory cortex. With this information, some yet unknown cortical mechanism is triggered that inhibits the tickling sensation from activating.

Interestingly, if the subsequent robotic touch is time delayed, even delayed by as little as one-fifth of a second, the subjects felt stronger touch sensations, similar to when the touch was not self-produced.

In short, you can't usually tickle yourself because there is no element of surprise. Your brain is using the various internal sensory data it has available to anticipate exactly what is going to happen based on your movements and visual data. When the anticipated reaction and the actual reaction line up, your brain diminishes or even sometimes completely discards the sensation as a result of that action. On the other hand, when someone else is tickling you, there are unexpected sensations on the skin and these can result in the tickling sensation being activated.

WHY CRACKERS HAVE HOLES

It turns out the holes exist for a reason, not just for decoration or for convenience in some manufacturing process, as one might expect. In actuality, without these holes, crackers wouldn't bake correctly. Holes allow steam to escape during cooking. This keeps the crackers flat, instead of rising like a normal biscuit as the steam tries to escape; these holes also help to properly crisp the crackers.

When crackers are made, dough is rolled flat in sheets. These sheets then travel under a mechanism containing "docker" pins that put the holes in the dough. The positioning and number of holes vary depending on the size and shape of the cracker. If the holes are too close together, the cracker will be extra dry and hard, due to too much steam escaping. If the holes are too far apart, parts of the cracker will rise and form little bubbles on the surface of the cracker, which is undesirable in most types of crackers.

BONUS FACT

The name "cracker" for crackers was coined by cracker pioneer Josiah Bent in 1801, *supposedly* after he accidentally burned a batch of what we now call crackers. As the crackers burned, they made a crackling noise, which inspired him to name them as such. Bent was also the one who pioneered the cracker as a snack food, rather than just selling it for sailors' rations as his competition were selling them for at the time. To make them popular as a snack food, he knew he'd have to improve on the flavor, so he experimented until he eventually came up with soda crackers, which were precursors to saltine crackers. By 1810, Bent's cracker business was incredibly successful, and the National Biscuit Company (Nabisco) eventually acquired it. Nabisco, using Bent's recipe, released the saltine cracker in 1876. Their slogan for this new cracker was "Polly wants a cracker?"

WHY MOVIE ADVERTISEMENT CLIPS ARE CALLED "TRAILERS"

The first movie trailers occurred, not at the beginning of films as they do today, but rather at the end. They were called "trailers" because the advertisements would be spliced directly on the end of the reels, so that the movie advertisement's film "trailed" the actual film.

The first known movie trailer to appear in a theater was in November of 1913. It was made by Nils Granlund, advertising manager of Marcus Loew theaters in the United States. The trailer was for the musical *The Pleasure Seekers*, which was shortly to open on Broadway. In this trailer, he included short clips of rehearsals of the musical. This idea caught on and trailers began appearing routinely after films. This was particularly the case with cartoon shorts and serials that would often end in climactic situations where you needed to watch the next episode in the serial or cartoon to see what would happen. Thus, these trailers, in particular that advertised the next episode, made a lot more sense at the end of the serial or cartoon than at the beginning.

However, it didn't take long for movie studios to realize that film advertisements would be a lot more effective if they showed up before the movie, instead of after, and by the end of the 1930s the switch had been made. Despite the industry's sincerest attempts over the last 60 or 70 years to get the name changed from "trailers" to some form of "previews," among industry professionals and English speaking audiences the world over, "trailer" is still a very popular term for these advertisements. Although, this has begun to change very recently among the general public when referring to trailers shown in theaters, which are now synonymously known as "previews."

BONUS FACT

While the first known trailer to appear in a theater was that listed above, Lou Harris, an executive at Paramount in the 1960s, states that the first trailer ever to show anywhere was at a New York area amusement park in 1912. One of the concessions workers at that park hung up a white sheet and showed the serial *The Adventures of Kathlyn*. At the end of the episode, Kathlyn is thrown into a lion's den. The concessions worker then spliced into the reel some film that showed the text, "Does she escape the lion's pit?" This simple text is considered to be the first ever rudimentary attempt at a trailer.

The first major trailer company was the National Screen Service. They began making crude film advertisements from transferred film stills without the permission of the film studios. They would then sell these film advertisements to be added on to the endings of films. Rather than sue this company and have them shutdown for their innovation, as studios would most certainly do today, the film industry chose to embrace this novel format for trailers and began providing the National Screen Service with film footage they could use in these advertisements. As a result, the National Screen Service secured a virtual monopoly on movie trailers for a time. It wasn't until the late 1920s that studios began commonly making trailers of their own.

WHY PEOPLE ON PLANES AND SHIPS USE THE WORD "MAYDAY" WHEN IN EXTREME DISTRESS

In 1923, a senior radio officer, Frederick Stanley Mockford, in Croydon Airport in London, England, was asked to think of one word that would be easy to understand for all pilots and ground staff in the event of an emergency.

The problem had arisen as voice radio communication slowly became more common, so an equivalent to the Morse code "SOS" distress signal was needed. Obvious a word like "help" wasn't a good choice for English speakers because it could be commonly used in normal conversations where no one was in distress.

At the time Mockford was considering the request, much of the traffic he was dealing with was between Croydon and Le Bourget Airport in Paris, France. With both the French and English languages in mind, he came up with the somewhat unique word "Mayday," the Anglicized spelling of the French pronunciation of the word "m'aider," which means "help me."

Four years later, in 1927, the International Radiotelegraph Convention of Washington made "Mayday" the official voice distress call used only to communicate the most serious level of distress, such as with life-threatening emergencies.

When using Mayday in a distress call, it is traditional to repeat it three times in a row, "Mayday, Mayday, Mayday." This is to make sure it is easily distinguishable from a message about a Mayday call and from any similar sounding phrases in noisy conditions or garbled transmissions.

In situations where a vessel merely requires assistance, but is not in grave and imminent danger, a distress call of "pan-pan" can be used instead. Essentially, it means you need aid, but you don't need support personnel to necessarily drop what they're doing right that instant and come help you, as with a Mayday.

Like Mayday, pan-pan is the Anglicized spelling of a French word, in this case "panne," which means "broken / failure / breakdown." Also, as with Mayday, one should state it three consecutive times: "pan-pan pan-pan pan-pan," followed by which station(s) you are addressing and your last known location, nature of your emergency, etc.

If there is no reply to a Mayday or pan-pan call by the Coast Guard or other emergency agency, and a couple minutes have passed since the last call, some other radio source, such as another ship or plane that received the call, should transmit their own Mayday call, but on behalf of the ship or plane that first made the call, repeating the pertinent information they heard when they received the Mayday message.

BONUS FACT

"SOS" was officially adopted during the 1906 Berlin Radiotelegraphic Conference. Today, it is commonly held that "SOS" is an acronym for "Save Our Ship" and thus often written "S.O.S." In actuality, "SOS" isn't an acronym for anything, which is why it is incorrect to put full stops between each letter.

So why was SOS chosen to signify a distress signal? This was explained in the 1918 Marconi Yearbook of Wireless Telegraphy and Telephony: "This signal [SOS] was adopted simply on account of its easy radiation and its unmistakable character. There is no special significance in the letters themselves..."

WHY GETTING KICKED IN THE TESTICLES CAUSES PAIN IN THE ABDOMEN

You may have wondered why getting kicked in the testes causes pain in the abdomen, as well as nausea, despite these areas not being directly physically impacted. Wonder no more!

Testes originally form in the abdomen near the stomach and kidneys. The nerves and blood vessels remain attached in that region, even after the balls drop. So when a guy gets kicked in the testes or otherwise has his sensitive bits squished, the pain involved travels up from each testicle into the abdominal cavity via the spermatic plexus, which is the primary nerve of each testicle, and then to the spine.

In addition to the pain in the stomach area, many men also experience severe nausea. This is thought to be caused by a huge rush of sympathetic nervous system discharge. So the body's tolerance level for that rush determines whether that person will be someone susceptible to actually vomiting when kicked in the testes.

BONUS FACT

Getting kicked or hit in the testes can actually damage a man's reproductive abilities. Further, if the force is severe enough, it can sometimes require removal of the testicle(s) itself. This, in turn, can cause other significant medical problems, especially if both need removed. Because of this, kicking or hitting a male in the testes in non-self-defense situations is considered sexual assault in many countries in the world.

WHY FERRIS WHEELS ARE CALLED "FERRIS WHEELS"

Before there were Ferris wheels, there were simply "pleasure wheels." Pleasure wheels weren't nearly as large as most Ferris wheels are today. Rather, they were just big enough to hold a few passengers who sat in chairs that were suspended from wooden rings, with the wheel turned manually from the ground.

Pietro Della Valle recorded one of the first known accounts of riding one of these early pleasure wheels. He was a Roman traveler who was visiting Constantinople during a Ramadan festival in 1615. At the festival, he decided to take a ride on the pleasure wheel to see what it was like: "I was delighted to find myself swept upwards and downwards at such speed. But the wheel turned round so rapidly that a Greek who was sitting near me couldn't bear it any longer, and shouted out 'Soni! Soni!' (enough! enough!)"

Pleasure wheels spread throughout Europe in the seventeenth century and made their way to America in 1848 when Antonio Maguino built one to attract visitors to a new fair in Georgia.

Nearly half a century later, in 1892, William Somers installed three fifty-foot wheels at Coney Island, Atlantic City, and Asbury Park. The giant wheels were a marvel at the time due to their extreme size. Somers was granted a patent for his ride, which he called a "Roundabout."

Sometime between the installation of the rides in 1892 and the middle of 1893, a soon-to-be-famous man sat on the wheel in Atlantic City. His name was George Washington Gale Ferris, Jr.

It had been announced that the World's Columbian Exposition would be held in Chicago in 1893, and the exposition's organizers challenged American engineers to come up with a structure for the fair that would be even better than the Eiffel Tower, which had been featured at the Paris International Exposition in 1889. They requested something "daring, original, and unique" to act as a monument at the fair.

Ferris, a graduate of Rensselaer Polytechnic Institute who got his start in the railroad industry before moving on to bridge building, was up for a challenge. Undoubtedly inspired by his ride on the Atlantic City Roundabout, Ferris proposed an even greater venture that he claimed would "Out-Eiffel Eiffel."

According to Ferris, he came up with the idea over dinner: "...down in a Chicago chop house... I hit on the idea. I remember remarking that I would build a wheel, a monster. I got some paper and began to sketch it out. I fixed the size, determined the construction, the number of cars we would run, the number of people it would hold...and my plan has never varied an item from that day."

At its completion, the very first Ferris wheel certainly was a monster. At 264 feet tall (80.46 meters), it was by far the largest attraction at the World's Columbian Exhibition that year. The wheel had 36 cars, each of which could carry 60 people, making the total carrying capacity a whopping 2,160 happy fair-goers at once. Nearly 40,000 people rode the Ferris wheel daily at the fair, each paying 50 cents (about $13 today) for a 20-minute ride. By the time the Ferris wheel was too old to carry more passengers, some 2.5 million people had ridden on it.

Of course, William Somers had something to say about Ferris's famed wheel, and in 1893 Ferris was slammed with a lawsuit. Somers claimed that Ferris had infringed on his patent, but the judge found that there were enough structural differences for the Ferris wheel to be an invention in its own right.

Given that Ferris's wheel was widely publicized and by far the largest at the time, even well over a century later, we're still calling such rides, regardless of who made them or their specific design, "Ferris wheels."

BONUS FACT

While the original Ferris wheel was destroyed in 1906 after it reached the end of its life-cycle, many other so-called Ferris wheels have, of course, continued to be made. The most famous of them all is probably the London Eye which sits on the edge of the Thames in London. The Eye opened to the public in 2000, and at that time it was the largest Ferris wheel in the world at an astounding 443 feet (135 meters) tall. However, other Ferris wheels have since surpassed it in size: the Star of Nanchang in China is 525 feet tall (160 meters), and the Singapore Flyer is 541 feet (165 meters) tall—as of the publishing of this book, it is the tallest in the world. That being said, there are plans in the works to create a massive Ferris wheel in Dubai that will be 689 feet (213 meters) tall and cost $1.6 billion to create, but construction isn't yet underway.

WHY MUSTARD IS YELLOW

A common misconception is that yellow mustard (the kind you put on your hot dog) is yellow because of the mustard seed. This is not true. The mustard seed is a dullish gray, brown color. The striking, bold yellow color actually comes from the rootstock of a plant called turmeric.

Turmeric, native to the rainy and humid tropical forests of South Asia, has been used as a natural food dye for centuries. The turmeric plant is harvested annually for its rhizome, or rootstock. The rhizome is boiled, dried, and ground into a powder. This powder is then mixed with mustard seed powder, vinegar, water, salt, and voila, you've got yourself traditional yellow mustard!

Turmeric is also a common ingredient in many South Asian and Indian dishes. It provides an earthy, slightly bitter taste that complements many curries. It began to make its way west during the twelfth and thirteenth centuries. In medieval England, turmeric was often called "Indian saffron" since it was used as a cheaper alternative to the much more pricey saffron. In the eighteenth century, turmeric was beginning to be grown in Caribbean countries, where the climate was similar to South Asia. Jamaica became a big grower of turmeric and to this day, rhizome powder is still used in Jamaican cuisine.

Getting back to the mustard of it all, mustard itself dates back to the ever-enterprising Romans. They would combine the seeds with unfermented grape juice to create what they called "burning juice," or "mustum ardens" in Latin (hence our now familiar English word "mustard"). The popularity of mustard grew in Rome and swept into their conquered territories. In the Burgundy region of France, most famous for its wines, a little town called Dijon embraced mustard and began making its own variety, substituting the unfermented grape juice with vinegar. To this day, Dijon, France, is still known as the mustard capital of the world for its unique and sharp tasting Dijon mustard.

Yellow mustard didn't come along until the turn of the twentieth century. In 1884, two brothers, Robert and George French, bought a flourmill in Rochester, New York, after their previous flourmill upstate burned down. They named the mill the R.T. French Company. When Robert passed away, George's other brother, Francis, came aboard to help the family business. In 1904, George began experimenting with "creamy salad mustard." He added turmeric to the traditional recipe for added presentation and color. Yellow mustard premiered at the St. Louis World's Fair in 1904 as a condiment to put on hot dogs to great fanfare. The rest, as it were, is mustard history.

BONUS FACT

Grey-Poupon, the world's most famous Dijon mustard, was created in 1777 by a partnership between Maurice Grey, a mustard maker with an unusual recipe calling for white wine, and Auguste Poupon, his financial backer. Grey-Poupon took off, not just because of the uniqueness of the recipe, but also because they were the first mustard makers to utilize an automatic mustard-making machine. Their original store still stands in downtown Dijon today.

WHY CUTTING ONIONS MAKES YOUR EYES WATER

Onions, along with many other plants in the Allium species (garlic is another popular one), absorb sulfur from the soil. When onions are chopped, cells within the onion break and release certain enzymes. These enzymes then react with the sulfur, creating amino acid sulfoxides. These, in turn, create the highly unstable syn-propanethial-S-oxide, which is a combination of sulfuric acid, sulfur dioxide, and hydrogen sulfide. When this substance, in a gaseous state, comes in contact with the moisture in your eye, it triggers a burning sensation via the ciliary nerve.

Tears in the eyes are regulated by the lachrymal gland, which is situated just above your eyelids. When the brain gets a message that there is an irritant in the eye, such as the above syn-propanethial-S-oxide, which gives a burning sensation, it then kicks the lachrymal glands into overdrive, trying to flush the irritant out of your eye(s) with tears.

Cooked onions won't produce this same effect because the process of cooking the onion inactivates the enzymes needed to make the syn-propanethial-S-oxide. So you can safely chew the cooked onions without getting teary-eyed.

ABOUT TODAYIFOUNDOUT.COM

TodayIFoundOut.com was founded based on the idea that it is always good to learn something new every day.

It was also partially inspired by the fact that there is a decided lack of "interesting fact / trivia" style books and websites out there where the facts presented are extremely well researched. From our experience, many such books and websites have just as many myths or misleading information presented as facts as they do actual facts.

Our goal is to raise the bar on that significantly, providing interesting content where you know everything has been highly researched by amazingly well credentialed authors including a couple with Juris Doctorates, a Ph.D., and several more with Master's degrees in various fields.

We have one guiding precept in all we do: provide extremely interesting, thoroughly researched content for people to feed their brains with.

ON ACCURACY

At TodayIFoundOut.com we strive to get all the facts perfectly accurate every time and with no exaggerations.

With that in mind, if you have found any potential error in this book, whether it be a simple typo or perhaps some point that you don't think is perfectly accurate, send us a message via: http://www.todayifoundout.com/index.php/contact-us/ so we can look into the matter and correct it if necessary. We're extremely obsessive about inaccuracies, so *please* don't hesitate.

We specifically chose the particular method of publication we did (print-on-demand and digital) so that. if, despite our sincerest efforts, any errors did slip through the various stages of fact checking, and re-checking (and then re-checking again), we could correct it immediately for anyone who purchases the book after the error is discovered.

We'll also be maintaining a list of corrections, if any, here: http://www.todayifoundout.com/index.php/wise-book-whys-addendum/

We're crossing our fingers that the "Corrections" portion of that page stays empty.

AUTHORS

This book features the work of seven of TodayIFoundOut.com's authors, listed below (for which authors wrote which specific topics go here: http://www.todayifoundout.com/index.php/wise-book-whys-addendum/)

Daven Hiskey: Daven has a B.S. and M.S. in Computer Science, a Web Programmers Certificate, and a fairly significant background in mathematics, physics, astronomy, history, literature, electrical engineering, and music, spending much of his time in college seeing if he could set a record for course credits, student loans, and years spent to achieve a single eight year B.S. degree that had little to do with a good portion of the classes he took. After the University (literally) forced him to graduate with a degree in something, he then found a loophole in their system by continuing on in a graduate program. After completing said program, he promptly started a website, TodayIFoundOut.com and has been doing that ever since.

Iuliia Glushchenko: Iuliia has a PhD in Sociology and has over eight years of teaching experience at the University of Dnipropetrovsk in the Ukraine.

Emily Upton: Emily is a graduate of Hollins University with a B.A. in English with a concentration in creative writing. In her free time, she likes to read, travel, cuddle koalas, and pat kangaroos. If you guessed she currently lives in Australia, you're correct.

Scott Hiskey: Scott is a long time paramedic and fire fighter who has particular expertise in the medical field and the human body in general. He also has an extensive background in physics, specializing in the fundamental forces.

Matt Blitz: Matt is a writer, comedian, and winner of multiple "good effort" ribbons. After finishing 53rd in the world in rock, paper, scissors, he went into hiding due to the fame such a distinction brings. He has since come out from hiding to find the world didn't change much in those 16 hours. Matt is also a field agent/writer/traveler for atlasobscura.com and Obscura Society LA.

Noah Wass: Noah has a B.S. in Plastics Engineering Technology that allows him to design and build all things polymer related. When he is not being an engineer, he is contributing to his bike blog, Bike In Review, writing articles for Today I Found Out, riding his bike or camping with his family (when the weather cooperates).

Terynn Boultan: Terynn has a B.S., as well as a B.E. degree. Her writing career began in elementary school with adventure stories starring her pet hamster, Montgomery. Now with three daughters of her own in elementary school, Terynn continues to write children's fiction and has entered the realm of blogging. She currently runs three blogs: deardaughters.ca, musingsofamom.net and themotherlists.com. She also, of course, writes articles for TodayIFoundOut.com.

ACKNOWLEDGMENTS

I would like to thank Samantha Gudger, Dusti Nielsen, Scott Hiskey, and C.J. Henderson for editing this book and catching many-a-typo and awkwardly worded sentence that my eyes seem to slide right passed.

Noreen who, besides doing most of the graphics work on TodayIFoundOut.com (including creating the infographics that helped infuse the site with that first bit of significant traffic), also helped design the cover of this book.

The various writers at TodayIFoundOut.com that have helped take it from a reasonably popular personal blog to a site that gets a couple million visitors per month.

Jon, owner of Dumpaday.com, who provides me with daily virtual "water cooler" talk as we've worked on building or websites from nothing to a couple of the more popular sites in the world.

And, finally, Simon Whistler for first emailing me with the idea of an audiobook for TodayIFoundOut.com featuring his prodigious vocal talents, which finally got me to buckle down and create the necessary content for such a work, with the result being *The Wise Book of Whys*.

Daven Hiskey
Gold Bar, Washington
November 2013

Made in the USA
Lexington, KY
27 May 2015